Learning vs Testing

Strategies That Bridge the Gap

Pat Wyman

A Complete Guidebook for Teachers and Parents

Zephyr Press

Chicago

Learning vs. Testing
Strategies That Bridge the Gap

Grades K–8

©2001 Pat Wyman
Printed in the United States of America

ISBN-13: 978-1-56976-120-5
ISBN-10: 1-56976-120-5

Published by Zephyr Press
An imprint of Chicago Review Press
814 North Franklin Street
Chicago, Illinois 60610
(800) 232-2187
www.zephyrpress.com

Library of Congress Cataloging-in-Publication Data

Wyman, Pat, 1950–
    Learning vs. testing: strategies that bridge the gap: a complete guidebook for
teachers and parents / Pat Wyman.
        p. cm.
    Includes bibliographical references.
    ISBN 1-56976-120-5
  1. Learning. 2. Cognitive styles. 3. Educational tests and measurements. I. Title:
Learning versus testing. II. Title

LB1060.W96 2000
  371.26—dc21   00-043336

Dedication

F or J. P. and all the gifted and special students who are disguised as "at risk, learning disabled, attention deficit disordered, dyslexic, below grade level, not up to potential," or for any other reason not making the grade in our schools. There are so many ways to help you radiate success. I pray we do whatever it takes to reach you.

Acknowledgments

I'd like to express my heartfelt gratitude to each person who helped create this book. It is a truly a work of partnership and love. My family has provided the love, encouragement, and support that helped me through many long days and nights. I thank you for your wisdom, love, honesty, and contributions—J. P., Erin, and Joseph. You are the guiding light in my life and I love you always.

To my dearest friends and extended family, there are never enough words to tell you how deeply grateful I am for your guidance, candor, and patient editing. You all listened to my questions, requests for help, and prayers with the same special kind of love and support you have always provided. You continue to bless my life and I thank you. For Joy, you spent so many days and precious hours on the phone providing me feedback, new ideas, information, and such truly amazing suggestions that I will never be able to thank you enough. To Elizabeth and Russell, you are beyond patient and kind. Your comments, intelligence, and practical ideas have contributed greatly to the book. Whitney, you will always be my "little angel." Thank you for being wise beyond your years. Jim, Teri, Adam, and Becky, your love is felt always. For Beth, the years have flown by and you have always been there when I needed you. This time, your help will forever be printed on the pages that reflect your knowledge and compassion for children. Tony, thank you for sharing yourself to show other children that they can have fun while learning. Lynn, Conrad, Anne, and Robbert, your spirit is reflected in so many words in the book and I thank you deeply for your blessings and providing so much direction and guidance. Tabatha, you freed me from so many other things; without your help this book could not have been written. You will always have a special place in my heart and I appreciate everything you do. Steve, your wisdom, encouragement, and commitment have been a tremendous inspiration to me. I thank you always. A special acknowledgement goes to Levi Miller, whose unique artistic creations have enhanced the book beyond words. Thank you for sharing your extraordinary talent.

I also offer my deepest thanks to Zephyr Press, which has been more than the publishers of the book. Your faith in me and your vision for the book is reflected on each of these pages. Thank you for sharing these "second chances" with all the children.

To the thousands of teachers who have taken my courses, attended my staff in-service workshops, and offered their hope, trust, and desire to try new things to help their students, I thank you forever.

And finally, to the innovators, pioneers, and guides—your work has contributed to the love and commitment you see on these pages. Thank you, Dr. J. P. Guilford, Mary Meeker, Colin Rose, Eric Jensen, Dr. Georgi Lozanov, Drs. Beth and Greg Gilman, John Robbins, Sheila Ostrander, Leslie Hart, David Sousa, Carla Hannaford, Dr. Candace Pert, Allen and Virginia Crane, Bob Williams, Dr. Joel Zaba, Marjie Thompson, Dr. Kristy Remick, Dr. Renate Nummela Caine, Geoffrey Caine, Marilyn Ferguson, James Kimple, Robert Dilts, Anthony Robbins, Dr. Valerie Maxwell, Frances Shapiro, Beth Slingerland, Dr. Madeline Hunter, Dr. Tony Buzan, Dr. Melvyn Werbach, Richard Bandler, John Grinder, Dr. Julian Whitaker, William Glasser, Dawna Markova, Robert Sylwester, Drs. Rita and Kenneth Dunn, Sam Graci, Bobbi DePorter, Marilee Sprenger, Joyce Wycoff, Dr. Jeannette Vos, Dr. Doris Rapp, Dr. Donald Lofland, Elizabeth Miles, Don Campbell, Win Wenger, Dane Spotts, Dr. Richard Restak, Dr. Ron Brandt, Dr. Marian Diamond, Robert Ornstein, Lynn Schroeder, David Lazear, and Dr. Jean Houston.

Contents

Foreword by Colin Rose   vii

Preface   x

Introduction: The Angels in Our Midst   xv

1 How Children Learn vs. How Schools Test   1

2 The Reading Solution—Foundations First Success Program   21

3 What You and Your School Can Do to Raise Reading Scores   33

4 Word Wizard—Vocabulary Mastery   55

5 Recipe for Super Spellers   67

6 Math Facts Mastery   79

7 Mind Matters   91

8 Magnificent Memory Strategies   101

9 Brain Smart—Body Smart   113

Epilogue—Some Thoughts for the Thoughtful   127

Bibliography   130

Resources   134

Foreword

O nce in a while a new book appears that makes a major
contribution to our understanding of how children learn
and how we can empower them to become successful, self-
sufficient, lifelong learners. This is a book you will want to
keep as a standard and use the strategies both in school and at
home. It will transform the life of every child it touches.

Because the information is aligned with the most recent
research on the brain, school districts can improve their students'
performance and integrate the strategies throughout their entire
curriculum. Parents will discover new ways to teach their
children how to learn in all subject areas.

Pat Wyman's unique discussion about the mismatch between learning and testing styles identifies a problem faced in
every school—how to help those students whose preferred
learning style does not match the written, visual tests they are
required to take. Her breakthrough is to not only identify why
many students receive poor grades and lower test scores but to
provide unique and refreshing solutions to such a long-standing
problem.

The reason many students face challenges in school lies in
the way tests are structured. The tests are, for the most part,
written. Moreover, they are increasingly based on multiple-
choice questions—because such exams are inexpensive to
grade, easy to standardize, and meet the increasing demand for
assessments, comparisons between schools, and national
progress benchmarks.

For a child with a linear and visual learning style, such tests
present few problems. But children with other learning prefer-
ences will be at a major disadvantage. This is because the way
they have been learning is at odds with the way they are now
being tested.

For example, students with a preference for kinesthetic learning who have stored their learning though physical means are now having to output that learning through a principally visual medium.

The practice of teaching directed to each child's unique form of intelligence (known as multiple intelligence teaching) has produced more sensitivity and motivation for the students as they learn. When exam time comes, however, non-visual students taught in their own style run up against a mismatch between how they have learned and the style in which they are being tested. And most have no strategies to cope. When they cannot translate into writing what they have learned in another style, they conclude that they are poor learners and a downward spiral of expectations commences.

This book contains many such strategies and is therefore invaluable for any student who wants to get better grades—and for every teacher who wants to provide his or her children with the means to cope with the sort of tests they will face throughout life.

Maybe, one day, we will design and use tests that are fairer, but Pat Wyman wisely does not hold her breath. The solution, she says, is to ensure that students are taught how to store and retrieve what they know in ways that make it possible to display that knowledge in written tests. This book contains many such strategies and is therefore invaluable for any student who wants to get better grades—and for every teacher who wants to provide his or her children with the means to cope with the sort of tests they will face throughout life.

But the book has an even more powerful subtext. Our pupils will not reach their real potential if we merely continue to focus on how to teach better. The real focus must be on empowering every student with a whole range of learning and memory strategies to meet a wide variety of learning situations—a palette of learning colors, a repertoire of learning moves, and a medley of learning voices. Only then will they become self-sufficient learners, fully able to capitalize, for example, on the enormous self-learning opportunities opened up by such new technologies as the Internet.

In a world where knowledge is commonly estimated to be doubling every few years and where jobs require constant reskilling, learning how to learn has become the essential underpinning skill of the truly educated person. The problem is that too many schools still only teach *what*, which can rapidly get out of date, when they should be teaching *how*, which is a skill for life.

Pat Wyman's book is an extraordinary gift to the key skill of the new economy—learning how to learn.

Colin Rose
Author, *Accelerated Learning*
and *Accelerated Learning for
the 21st Century*
England
May 2000

Preface

This is a book about second chances . . .
. . . second chances for our children and second chances for teachers and parents to help every child succeed in our schools. On these pages you will find a new model of learning and a fresh start for the millions of students who happen to learn very differently from how they are tested in school.

The children in our schools have an extraordinary capacity to learn in many different styles. They may learn through their visual sense by seeing, their auditory sense by hearing, or their physical sense using a hands-on approach. Yet, when it comes to assessing that learning, most schools limit their testing format to just one of those styles.

The traditional, written tests that most schools give to measure student progress cater to students with strong visual *learning traits.*

The traditional, written tests that most schools give to measure student progress cater to students with strong *visual* learning traits. Students who learn and think best in pictures form the associations needed to retrieve information quickly and accurately for their written tests. These students have a natural learning strength, which matches the school's highly visual learning and testing environment. They easily make images from the words they hear and read, they are usually neat and organized, they take notes well, and their mental images rapidly trigger the words they need during a written test. Students who prefer to learn in this style tend to have higher grades and test scores that reflect the match between their learning and testing style.

There are, however, millions of students who prefer to learn in other styles, such as auditory or kinesthetic. For these students a mismatch occurs between how they learn, store, and retrieve information and the way in which they are required to output what they have learned—on written tests. These written tests may be multiple choice, short answer, essay, or standardized. The learning and memory processes required to answer the questions are quite similar.

Students who have stored the material they have learned in styles that are not aligned with the type of test they are taking often find they either cannot translate what they know into written form or they cannot retrieve the information quickly enough to form their answers. When they attempt to use an auditory or kinesthetic modality to retrieve and write down information for these tests, they are often frustrated and hindered in their efforts due to the mismatch involved. This mismatch will not allow them to "show what they know" easily and heavily contributes to their lower grades, and may even be a cause of poor test scores nationwide.

When they attempt to use an auditory or kinesthetic modality to retrieve and write down information for these tests, they are often frustrated and hindered in their efforts due to the mismatch involved.

My son, J. P., is a wonderful example of a person who prefers to learn in a single style and who often struggles to convert his knowledge into writing. He is a true kinesthetic learner and seems to love his tactile sense over all others. He needs to move around nearly all the time and doesn't naturally make the pictures in his mind to "see" what organization looks like. His crumpled papers generally reflect that he has touched and made contact with the material on them.

When allowed to demonstrate his understanding of new material in a hands-on manner, he performs quite well. One year, he built an excellent model showing how the plates of the earth shift during an earthquake. He placed two paper "plates" on top of his amplifier and played a low base sound on his electric guitar. The plates separated due to the vibration, and the model easily demonstrated how the plates move during an earthquake. Although he got an A on his demonstration, he could not find the correct words to describe the process and answer questions on it for the written test. He received an overall grade of C on the test, even though his teacher was certain he "knew" the information.

While his memory of what was learned was stored in a sensory-motor pattern in his brain, J. P. was not able to gain access to it and convert it into words for the written test. For all practical purposes, he had only a "physical sense" of the information and had not linked it to the pictures and associations needed to trigger the words required to pass the written test.

Like J. P., many children may not be able to convert their physical, experiential knowledge into writing during traditional testing. It is not a function of ignorance of the information but of not knowing how to access and translate the information into writing.

> *J. P.'s experience is an example of a conflict between how students learn and how they are tested. This conflict also creates a serious dilemma for teachers.*

When J. P. was allowed to use his learning preference, he demonstrated his knowledge of the shifting earthquake plates. However, he did not acquire or store the same knowledge using other, more visual brain pathways that would have allowed him to earn a better grade on his written test, which contained multiple choice, short answer, and essay questions. J. P.'s experience is an example of a conflict between how students learn and how they are tested. This conflict also creates a serious dilemma for teachers. For many years, teachers have been trained in a theory known as multiple intelligences (MI). The theory of multiple intelligences, developed in the early 1980s by Dr. Howard Gardner (*Frames of Mind* 1983), expanded on Dr. J. P. Guilford's original and groundbreaking work on human intelligence (Guilford 1950, 1967).

Teachers trained in the multiple intelligences tradition are taught to design different types of lesson plans for eight or more types of intelligences and teach students to access all eight of their ways of knowing. Problems arise for both teachers and students when most districts still require single modality, written, and standardized tests to be the primary measurements for student progress. Today, teachers are being held accountable for those test results.

For all practical purposes, the many clashes between multiple intelligence teaching and single-modality testing place both students and teachers in a significant quandary: If a child's preferred learning strength does not correspond directly with the testing method of choice, that child may suffer needlessly from low grades and low self-esteem. To complicate matters, neither school districts nor employers have (nor likely will) create tests suited to their students' or employees' preferred learning styles.

> *If a child's preferred learning strength does not correspond directly with the testing method of choice, that child may suffer needlessly from low grades and low self-esteem.*

Learning vs. Testing—Strategies That Bridge the Gap was written to dissolve the dilemma that both teachers and students face and solve the mismatch between learning and testing styles. It will give you unique and practical strategies to help students learn *how* to learn and process information in ways that more closely match how they will be assessed. This book is intended to help raise student grades and test scores in reading, spelling, math facts, vocabulary, and other subject areas. The strategies can be used throughout the curriculum and will transform your teaching as well how your students learn.

You will find that this book bridges the gap between how many students learn and how they are tested. These strategies are meant to give newfound hope to struggling students who want to raise their grades, and to give teachers who want to raise test scores to meet higher standards the answers they have been looking for. The strategies you will find in this book are solidly based on over 25 years of my research, practice, and experience with students of all ages. The information combines the best available scientific information from the fields of neuroscience, psychology, medicine, psychiatry, optometry, environmental medicine, and with the insights and methods of several instructional models.

The methods in this book form a program I call A.C.E.S., Accelerating Children's Excellence in School. The strategies offered here are designed to bring out the best in all students and show them new ways of accelerating their success.

During the past 12 years, teachers attending my teacher-education classes or taking my courses on video have applied these strategies in their own classrooms and documented their students' pre- and post-test progress. Using these techniques, they have documented that they have successfully raised the grades of a very high percentage of their students.

As long as grades remain the yardstick by which teachers and children are measured, I believe our students deserve to receive the knowledge and strategies they need to achieve excellent marks. Devoting just a brief course at the beginning of each school year on "how to learn and how to test" methods would result in students acquiring skills they need to continue to learn for a lifetime.

—Pat Wyman, M.A.

Introduction
The Angels in Our Midst

*I believe the children are our future. Teach them well
and let them lead the way.*

> —Whitney Houston,
> from "Greatest Love of All" (Arista Records)

It was the first day of school. I was fresh out of my teacher-
training program and not a single class had prepared me for
what I was about to see and do.

The school was a junior high, a middle school of about
2,000 seventh, eighth, and ninth graders. It was in the middle
of a Los Angeles ghetto area and the school seemed like a
prison. There were security guards with weapons attached to
their bodies. All I knew for sure was that the male students
were much taller and bigger than I was. Nobody had mentioned
this fact during my teacher education classes.

I had applied for this job because I loved kids and wanted
to teach them how to read. I had been told that most of the
students were reading several years below grade level and
progress was very slow. The principal gave me a job during my
interview (I'm sure she was desperate) and promptly assigned
me five reading classes of 30 students each. This meant that I
would see 150 students a day who were reading around the
second-, third-, and fourth-grade levels, even though they were
in junior high. And, oh yes. Most of my students belonged to
three major street gangs—18th Street, Bloods, and Crips.

If ever there was a place where all the odds were stacked
against these students learning anything—this was it. In fact, I
immediately began to doubt everything about myself and whatever abilities I might have thought I had. How could I ever

teach anyone anything—let alone reading? Everyone seemed to have an endless list of reasons why these kids were not reading. They had a bad home life, they lived in the streets, they spoke another language, their parents did not care, and the rival gangs would kill them if they so much as walked on the wrong turf.

On that first day, the placement testing began in the reading department. The policy was to test all students and place them into classes of the same ability levels. I tested them for days, until all of us were exhausted.

On the final testing day, I watched one young man, whose name was Angel, simply fill in bubbles randomly on the scoring sheet without even reading the questions. Angel looked like the kind of person who had given up on school years ago. And from what I was told, school had certainly given up on him. I wondered how many Angels I had missed in the days before that. At the end of the period, I asked him to stay a minute after the other kids had left.

> *Angel looked like the kind of person who had given up on school years ago. And from what I was told, school had certainly given up on him.*

Angel glared down at me, all six feet, two inches of him. He was nearly a foot taller than I was and very angry looking. All the other teachers had told me to never smile during the first month or the kids would think I was soft. I looked up at Angel, and I smiled.

"You look really smart to me, and I noticed that you just marked any answers on the sheet without reading the questions. (I was sure he thought I was mentally out to lunch.) I promise not to tell any of your friends if you stay after school and take this test again. I'm sure you could be in any reading group you choose, if you spend a few minutes retaking the test. Here, I'll just throw this one away, and no one will ever know."

Angel stared at me and turned as if he were going to leave. But then, he turned back around and said he'd come back after school, but made it very clear that none of his friends were to know.

I did not know if I had made a mistake (what if Angel could not read at all?) and I was uneasy all day. But, no matter what, I felt that Angel deserved a second chance. School was clearly a place where he was lost, and I wanted to help change that for him. If I could reach him in some special way and provide another chance to show what he did know, he might actually want to be here every day. At lunch, I asked some of the other teachers about him, and was not surprised to learn that he had been in nothing but trouble since coming to the junior high.

Helping (Angel) to become a leader in school might make the difference between success and failure for him.

Angel did show up after school, and I gave him the test again. This time, he read the questions and filled in all the bubbles. I scored his test on the scantron machine while he waited. Excitedly, I told him that he had made a perfect score. He gave me the strangest look, mostly disbelief, and we went through the answers one by one to prove to him that he'd made 100 percent. I told him that he would be in my highest reading group. I also asked him if he would help me with the rest of the class. In a very few words, he agreed and left.

What I did not say to Angel was that my highest group was achieving around the fourth-grade level. I knew that Angel needed to learn to believe in himself and develop the confidence in his ability to succeed throughout the coming years, if we were to keep him in school and hopefully guide him in a more positive direction. Angel was like so many other students in the school. They were never tested to determine whether they had the visual skills needed to be able to read and had been passed on from grade to grade, because there seemed to be no other options. Helping him to become a leader in school might make the difference between success and failure for him.

I soon learned that Angel was one of the leaders in the 18th Street Gang. However, he also turned out to be the guardian angel I would need during my first year at the junior high. He kept me going (and unharmed) more than once, and taught me more about kids and life than any book ever could have. He inspired me to continue when times got very rough and helped me form a foundation for what teaching truly means.

Angel is typical of a student who never got a chance to show his capabilities. His story points out the fact that many students have hidden potential that can be invisible to teachers.

> *I knew that Angel needed to learn to believe in himself and develop the confidence in his ability to succeed throughout the coming years, if we were to keep him in school and hopefully guide him in a more positive direction.*

That potential can remain unrealized unless we give students second and third chances. Angel was unusual, however, in the sense that he had the ability to learn basic skills despite all that was stacked against him. Many other students will never reach even his skill level without the help and guidance of educators.

Our student dropout rates are staggering—no one knows how many Angels we lose every day and how many Angels never get the chance to succeed in the one place that we insist they go to day after day. We have scored them and ranked them and maybe even scared them—and all of us have lost. Millions of their test scores are lower every year, and our prison population continues to grow. In a system that requires mastery of written tests, our students must be given the skills they need to master these tests, or the progress we say we want will be greatly hindered.

None of us has made the grade when our children fail. Could it be that our fundamental teaching, learning, and testing process needs to change? Maybe we've been looking at the wrong standards—those of student measurements instead of how we teach and how we measure our own ability to reveal the gifts of each student. If our system chooses not to change, we must at least show all our students *how* to learn and teach them strategies to succeed at all of our required tests.

Angel gave me a second chance to evaluate what teaching and learning is all about. I began to have many questions about a system that sorts and categorizes students based on numbers. Angel was not a number rotating through the revolving door of school. He helped me look beyond the "test results" and into the heart of who a student really is. He truly inspired me to help students discover new ways to master what is asked of them in school, because doing so would help them understand that their grades are not who they really are.

I thank you forever, Angel, wherever you might be...for teaching me about the souls of the kids on whom school and society have given up. You taught me that when given a second chance, every student can succeed. Angel did succeed and in the two years he attended the junior high, he raised his reading grade level by nearly four years.

This book is for all the gifted Angels, disguised as learning disabled or "at risk." There are so many ways to help these students radiate success and achieve their best in our schools.

Chapter 1

How Children Learn
vs How Schools Test

In This Chapter

- **How Children Learn**

- **The Road from Learning to Testing**

- **Learning Strategies for Three Learning Styles**

- **Personal Learning Styles Inventory**

- **The Mismatch Mix-Up**

- **Mending the Mix-Up**

- **Matching Learning to Testing**

How
Children Learn

Mrs. Shane's class had spent the past several days learning about the Declaration of Independence. Her students read about it in their books, listened to her talk about it in class, did various projects on it for homework, and shared information in group activities. All of her students were present during the instructional period, all did the work in class and at home, and all took part in the small group activities. Mrs. Shane gave *her students a written test on the material and began to grade the papers. The test contained some essay, short-answer, and multiple-choice questions.*

When Mrs. Shane finished grading the papers she was very surprised to discover that her students' grades ranged from As to Fs. As she sat at home grading the papers she wondered why. "Why didn't they all get an A?" she thought. "It seemed as if they all knew the material during class."

> *"Why didn't they all get an A?" she thought. "It seemed as if they all knew the material during class."*

Most teachers can easily relate to Mrs. Shane's bewilderment. Actually, the answer lies in the difference between *how* her students learned and stored the material they studied, and what they *did* to retrieve it when they were tested in writing. Each student did something different as they tried to recall and write down the information on the test.

THE ROAD FROM LEARNING TO TESTING

In your classroom is a magnificent mix of students who learn in every possible way. Children have natural modalities or learning senses through which they process incoming information. They prefer to use certain modalities when learning (input), storing (storage), and recalling (output) what was learned. These modalities are known as visual, auditory, and kinesthetic.

Each of these modalities will provide specific gifts and challenges in the school environment (Markova 1992). Although many researchers have theorized about learning styles or many different types of intelligences, the most useful styles for the discussion on learning and testing are the visual, auditory, and kinesthetic styles described on page 5.

How can you use this information on learning-style modalities to help your students achieve higher grades and better results?

Visual—Auditory—Kinesthetic

In your class, some children prefer to be like movie-makers, "projecting pictures" of every word you say and everything they read on the movie screen in their head. These children are known as *visual learners*.

Some children will learn best by "listening," and are able to repeat it back to you as if there's a tape recorder in their mind. When they read, they hear the words in their head. These children are known as *auditory learners*.

Some children will get a "feel" for what they see and hear and want to have a "grip" on the material. They learn best through hands-on physical methods such as touching, feeling, or experiencing the material they are trying to learn. These children are known as *kinesthetic learners*.

Of course, no child learns in only one style and most children will use some of each style as they go through each day. However, in my experience, when learning and testing, most children prefer to rely on just one of those styles.

Knowing your students' preferred learning styles works like magic:

- To help them improve performance in school and on the job
- To teach them to learn faster and easier
- To enhance communication and rapport

One way to begin to find out how your students learn is to listen to how they speak. Their words will give distinct clues as to the style they are using.

- Visual style—"I see, I get the picture, that looks right."
- Auditory style—"I hear you, that rings a bell, that clicks."
- Kinesthetic style—" I feel, get a grip, I get it."

The next step to discovering students' preferred learning style is to be on the lookout for telltale traits.

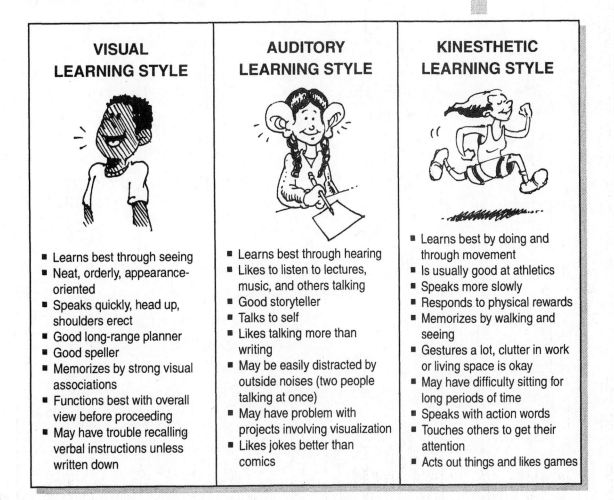

VISUAL LEARNING STYLE

- Learns best through seeing
- Neat, orderly, appearance-oriented
- Speaks quickly, head up, shoulders erect
- Good long-range planner
- Good speller
- Memorizes by strong visual associations
- Functions best with overall view before proceeding
- May have trouble recalling verbal instructions unless written down

AUDITORY LEARNING STYLE

- Learns best through hearing
- Likes to listen to lectures, music, and others talking
- Good storyteller
- Talks to self
- Likes talking more than writing
- May be easily distracted by outside noises (two people talking at once)
- May have problem with projects involving visualization
- Likes jokes better than comics

KINESTHETIC LEARNING STYLE

- Learns best by doing and through movement
- Is usually good at athletics
- Speaks more slowly
- Responds to physical rewards
- Memorizes by walking and seeing
- Gestures a lot, clutter in work or living space is okay
- May have difficulty sitting for long periods of time
- Speaks with action words
- Touches others to get their attention
- Acts out things and likes games

LEARNING STRATEGIES FOR THREE LEARNING STYLES

Once you know your students and their preferred learning styles, here are some things you can use as you teach, which are proven to work best for each style.

For the Visual Style—
Picture maps, diagrams, books, overheads, make mental movies

For the Auditory Style—
Lectures, dramatic reading, rhymes, music, make tapes, summarize aloud, teach others aloud

For the Kinesthetic Style—
Move about while reading or listening, learn in groups, create games, make notes and arrange on poster board, act out material being learned

Educational experts have long agreed that teachers can reach more students when they "enter their world." For example, when talking with your students, you will increase their understanding if you use visual, auditory, or kinesthetic words that match their styles of learning.

When you acknowledge the styles in which your students prefer to learn, you can design some of your lessons to accommodate each style. Students will be more attentive and more likely to complete assignments when given options that match their particular style of learning.

To find out how all your students choose to learn, on pages 8–9 is a *Personal Learning Styles Inventory* that I designed and have used for many years. A scoring key is included for you. If you would like your students to take the inventory online and let the computer score it giving percentages in each section, have them visit the website at ***www.howtolearn.com.***

> *Educational experts have long agreed that teachers can reach more students when they "enter their world."*

> *Students will be more attentive and more likely to complete assignments when given options that match their particular style of learning.*

PERSONAL LEARNING STYLES INVENTORY

Check only those boxes on the statements you agree with.

❑ 1. I prefer to hear a book on tape rather than reading it.

❑ 2. When I put something together, I always read the directions first.

❑ 3. I prefer reading to hearing a lecture.

❑ 4. When I am alone, I usually play music, hum, or sing.

❑ 5. I like playing sports more than reading books.

❑ 6. I can always tell directions like north and south no matter where I am.

❑ 7. I love to write letters or in a journal.

❑ 8. When I talk, I like to say things like, "I hear you, that sounds good, that clicks, or that rings a bell."

❑ 9. My room, desk, car, or house is usually disorganized.

❑ 10. I love working with my hands and building or making things.

❑ 11. I know most of the words to the songs I listen to.

❑ 12. When others are talking, I usually create images in my mind of what they are saying.

❑ 13. I like sports and think I am a pretty good athlete.

❑ 14. It's easy to talk for long periods of time on the phone with my friends.

❑ 15. Without music, life isn't any fun.

❑ 16. I am very comfortable in social groups and can usually strike up a conversation with almost anyone.

❑ 17. When looking at objects on paper, I can easily tell whether they are the same, no matter which way they are turned.

❑ 18. I usually say things like, "I feel, I need to get a handle on it, or get a grip."

❑ 19. When I recall an experience, I mostly see a picture of it in my mind.

❑ 20. When I recall an experience, I mostly hear the sounds and talk to myself about it.

❑ 21. When I recall an experience, I mostly remember how I felt about it.

❑ 22. I like music more than art.

Learning vs. Testing ©2001, Zephyr Press

❑ 23. I often doodle when I am on the phone or in a meeting.

❑ 24. I prefer to act things out rather than write a report on them.

❑ 25. I like reading stories more than listening to stories.

❑ 26. I usually speak slowly.

❑ 27. I like talking better than writing.

❑ 28. My handwriting is not usually neat.

❑ 29. I generally use my finger to point when I read.

❑ 30. I can multiply and add quickly in my head.

❑ 31. I like spelling and think I am a good speller.

❑ 32. I get very distracted if someone talks to me when the TV is on.

❑ 33. I like to write down instructions that people give me.

❑ 34. I can easily remember what people say.

❑ 35. I learn best by doing.

❑ 36. It is hard for me to sit still for very long.

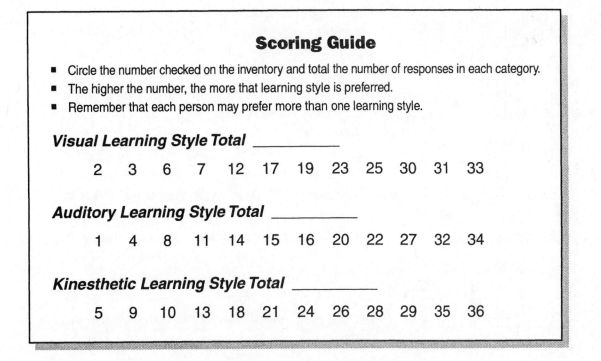

Scoring Guide

- Circle the number checked on the inventory and total the number of responses in each category.
- The higher the number, the more that learning style is preferred.
- Remember that each person may prefer more than one learning style.

Visual Learning Style Total _____

    2   3   6   7   12   17   19   23   25   30   31   33

Auditory Learning Style Total _____

    1   4   8   11   14   15   16   20   22   27   32   34

Kinesthetic Learning Style Total _____

    5   9   10   13   18   21   24   26   28   29   35   36

> *Let your students know that each person uses some of each style as they learn, store, and recall information, but that students may prefer one style over the others.*

Once you determine which style each student prefers, teach each of them about the characteristics of their own and the other two styles (page 5). These are described below. Let your students know that each person uses some of each style as they learn, store, and recall information, but that students may prefer one style over the others.

More importantly, show your students how school can be a very visual place (reading, writing, testing, and so on). Help them realize that adding some visual strategies to whichever style they prefer will help them perform better on their written tests. (You will read more about adding visual strategies on page 14.) Students should know that improving visual skills will be helpful when taking written tests.

THE MISMATCH MIX-UP

For many students, a major problem arises when the style in which they learn best does not match the written style most often used for testing. Additionally, a student may be inconsistent and use one style for some subjects and a different one for others. For example, you might have a student who is doing very well in reading but poorly in math. Possibly, that student is using the visual learning strategy in reading, and switching to a kinesthetic strategy during math. From my experience, I can say that students who perform well in math use a very visual style, creating and retrieving images of the material. This is very efficient when taking a written test.

When I was in high school, without realizing it, I used a visual-imaging strategy to help me get good grades in nearly every subject. However, when I first began taking geometry I had trouble with the concepts. One day, my teacher declared aloud that I was "stupid and would never understand geometry." He said this in front of the class, just before handing me a test with a D on it.

Based on this negative experience, I unintentionally switched learning styles and used one in math that did not work very well. I had created a mismatch mix-up between my learning style and the written testing style.

This mismatch was not related to my intelligence or desire to get a good grade. If a teacher had explained to me that adding a visual strategy in math would have been a better fit for math and help me get a higher grade, I would have gladly done it.

The mismatch in learning and testing styles can easily be likened to school sports. Imagine the frustration of a ninth-grader trying out for the school baseball team. As he steps up to the plate, bat in hand, he takes his stance, and pulls back the bat. At that moment, the coach yells,

"Wait! Put the bat down, come over here and write down for me how you would hit the ball and answer these questions about the game. Based on what you write, I will let you know if you make the team."

The mismatch between what this youngster knew (how to hit a ball) and how he was being tested on it (in writing) may seem absurd, but it actually happens in a similar way in classrooms every day.

According to recent brain research, there are separate brain areas that specialize in hearing, seeing, speaking, and generalizing words. (National Research Council 1999).

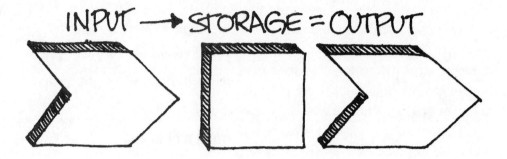

INPUT → STORAGE = OUTPUT

Additional brain research tells us which parts of the brain are activated during encoding (input) and which parts are activated during successful retrieval of both visual and semantic (word) memory. Imagery associated with words is more effortlessly and efficiently recalled (Iidaka 2000; Buckner 1996; Brewer 1998).

Teaching different types of learning and test-taking strategies to your students will empower them throughout their lifetime.

Thus, students learning new information in a physical or auditory style may not be able to show what they know. This is because their choice of strategies during learning and recall is not the most effective for achieving excellence on a written test.

Students may be trained in how to use pictures with associated words in order to maximize their performance on written tests. In addition, teaching different types of learning and test-taking strategies to your students will empower them throughout their lifetime. Students who rely on just one strategy or approach that does not yield the results they want might become stuck in a rut, which implies that they have "failed."

When students have a broader range of learning and testing strategies from which to select, they can tailor their approaches to the demands of specific circumstance (National Research Council 1999). Research by Marian Diamond and others in 1998, strongly supports the concept that innate characteristics of individuals are less important in performance than the training and encouragement they receive.

When the focus is on achieving higher grades and test scores, you will want to model those who have already achieved excellence.

There is much brain and learning research to be done, and many questions remain unanswered. I believe one of the issues most relevant to educators is the use of strategies. I concur with the evaluation by the National Research Council and National Academy of Sciences that, given the proper conditions, most individuals are capable of excellent performance (1991).

When the focus is on achieving higher grades and test scores, you will want to model those who have already achieved excellence. Look to students who get the best results and discover the strategies they use.

MENDING THE MIX-UP
Maximizing Learning with Diverse Strategies

When you teach students various strategies for learning and testing, they are far more likely to be efficient, successful learners and do well in the school environment, according to the Commission on Behavioral and Social Sciences and Education, a division of the National Research Council.

Research by the National Academy Press in 1999 also reveals that students will be able to select from a variety of strategies to solve problems, recognize which strategy will apply to the learning/testing situation, and transfer their strategies to new situations across the curriculum.

I am advocating we alter our teaching to better match the testing methods we choose, whenever possible. Determine how you will test your students, then match their input, storage, and output of the material in the same way.

■ If you give a test out loud, have the students study and rehearse the material aloud.

■ If you give your test by allowing students to act things out or use other physical methods to demonstrate that they know the material, have the students learn and study the material in the same way.

■ When you decide to test in writing, make certain that students are making visual images as they learn the material so they can retrieve these later during the test. Have your students rehearse the test in writing while making visual images to enhance long-term memory.

MATCHING LEARNING TO TESTING

You can easily help a child match their learning to the testing style by using certain strategies. By using strategies consciously, children become more active, self-sufficient, and successful learners.

Here are some strategies to match learning styles to written testing styles for visual, auditory, and kinesthetic learners. You can dramatically increase your students' learning and testing power by adding other learning strategies to their preferred style.

Visual Strategies for Written Tests

When I first began teaching in the early 1970s in Los Angeles, mentor teachers guided me in teaching methods that resulted in extraordinary success for my students. I was curious why they worked so well. I have since discovered that the secret to their success is exactly what the current brain research confirms. These methods helped the students learn how to *visualize* or make pictures of what they read or heard. Students who made mental pictures and associations recalled large amounts of material with excellent comprehension. They did this more quickly and accurately than other students and also got higher grades and test scores.

Neither my traditional teacher training nor specialist certificate programs actually taught me *how* to show my students to visualize. I learned many visual-memory and visualization activities to do with my students, but none were consistently successful. This was because I did not know the *how* of teaching my students to create and retrieve visual memories. Early on, I made many mistakes by telling my students to visualize what they were reading or visualize what we were talking about, but did not show them how to do this. I was inadvertently creating a mismatch for many of them between how they learned best and how I communicated to them.

Figuring out how to show my students to make mental images was an exciting journey. I observed lessons taught by other teachers, took many classes, read several psychology and medical information books on mental imagery, and interviewed various educational experts. Only then did the answers finally come.

Neither my traditional teacher training nor specialty certificate programs actually taught me how *to show my students to visualize.*

At the time, I had many students who made letter and word reversals when they read. To help them, I used a multi-modality approach known as the Slingerland method (Slingerland 1996). My students would look up, write their letters or words in the air, and say the words aloud. I also had them create their letters in a larger size and imagine them in different colors.

When it came time to write (or read), I noticed that the students would look back up as if seeing the letters or words in the air. In other words, they were checking to see if their actual work matched the visual image of what they had practiced previously. This worked very well and they no longer made letter or word reversals when they read or wrote.

Although this visual-memory method worked well with my special reading students, I wasn't clear whether it would work for all my students. So I interviewed and observed my highly visual students—these were the students who made the highest grades in the class.

Long before the current brain research could support the answers they gave, I discovered that they all used the same strategy, both when learning and remembering things for their tests. I learned that when they read, they *looked up* and naturally made images or pictures of what they were reading. These students seemed to know instinctively how to visualize.

They told me it was as if they were creating their own movie, as they converted everything to images in their mind. As I observed them during the act of learning and testing, the students read a bit and then looked in an upward direction as they processed the information. Some students closed their eyes as they processed, but still looked up. They told me this meant they were converting what they read into pictures.

Eyes and Their Signals

Although I did not understand why at the time, the physical act of *looking up* helped my students create and recall a kind of mental snapshot. They found that they could easily rely on these images, movies, or snapshots when they wanted to recall information. The actually used their upward eye movements to imagine a screen or other screen-like object in the air, and projected their images onto that screen.

Although I did not understand why at the time, the physical act of looking up *helped my students create and recall a kind of mental snapshot.*

As I sought out more information, I found that some classic research had been done in the late 1960s and early 1970s by A. Pavio and others. They had concluded that students using imagery had significantly better recall and faster response times to questions than those who did not.

In one of Pavio's studies (1969), students given long lists of pictures and long lists of words to remember scored far higher on recall of lists with pictures, thus supporting the power of visual memory. This classic research further noted that recall is enhanced by presenting information in both visual and verbal form together, and has been supported by more recent work (Clark 1991).

A few years after this research appeared, others expanded on it by observing that various eye movements appear to be tied to the visual, auditory, and kinesthetic learning modalities.

A field outside of education developed, known as neurolinguistics, and has been reported on in the recent works of Bobbi DePorter (1992, 1999).

When people are asked to recall pictures or asked to recall words, their eyes move to various positions during the process.

In addition, new psychological therapies to overcome stress and trauma make extensive use of eye movements to help patients successfully reprocess a traumatic event (Shapiro 1997). In a therapy known as Eye Movement Desensitization and Reprocessing (EMDR), patterned eye movements are used to remove or clear emotional, cognitive, and physical blockages (Parnell 1997).

Studies definitively have shown that eye movements trigger certain brain functions and are sensitive to task differences. In other words, there is an eye-brain relationship. When people are asked to recall pictures or asked to recall words, their eyes move to various positions during the process (Buckner 1996). As we create and store visual images in our minds the eyes move to a specific location (usually an upward left or upward right direction), activating certain areas in the brain. You can also observe the same thing in relation to other learning modalities. For example, notice what people do with their eyes when they recall sounds or access their feelings about something. Eye movements to the side (by the ear) will be used when recalling something said, and people generally look down when accessing feelings.

Without realizing it, my students helped me understand why children get such different grades on written tests even when they have all prepared in the same way beforehand. Those students who had problems during the test simply needed to learn how to make pictures in their mind when they studied and recall those same pictures as they took their written tests. Since exams are mostly given in the visual, written learning style, visual input, storage, and retrieval strategies work best for those types of exams.

Teachers can now use this eye-movement research to show their students how to create the mental images they need to reinforce and easily recall what they have learned.

How to Use the Visual Eye-Brain Connection for Written Tests

You can teach your students to add visual learning and visual-memory strategies as they learn and recall new information. In order to do this you will need to ask some questions that reveal which direction he or she looks to when recalling a visual image.

When your students look upward for visual memory, it is as if they have an internal blackboard or movie screen in their mind. Ask your students questions, that require them to access a picture. It is important that you continue asking these questions until your student looks up to the *left* or up to the *right*. Use the following examples so that each student *must* get a picture in his or her mind in order to answer the questions.

> *When your students look upward for visual memory, it is as if they have an internal blackboard or movie screen in their mind.*

- Get a picture of your best friend in your mind. Tell me exactly how he or she looks. What color are his or her hair, eyes, and so on? What does his or her favorite jacket look like?
- What was your mother, friend, or teacher wearing yesterday? Get a picture in your mind and tell me what color shirt or other clothing item he or she wore.
- Describe your favorite movie to me. Tell me exactly how a character or scene looked. What were the characters wearing, where were they when a certain event happened? Describe the location.

Visual-memory eye movements are not the same for every person. You must determine whether it is *up* to their left or *up* to their right. (This is easier to determine when you do not tell the person ahead of time what you are looking for.)

UP LEFT VISUAL MEMORY

UP RIGHT VISUAL MEMORY

If you have several students, record their visual memory locations with an *L* or *R* by their names in the roll book so you will be able to remind them of their eye-movement "visual memory" location when you want them to recall information in picture form. It will either be up left or up right for each student.

Now, when you teach anything that requires visual memory (such as spelling, math facts, reading comprehension, pictures of the story, science, vocabulary, and so on), you can actually use that eye movement information to physically place the word or information to be learned either up to the left or up to the right, so that retrieval is consistently successful.

You will be showing the students how to access visual memory by having them use their eye movements to see a picture in their mind. You can also get your students "looking up" by making use of overhead projectors and placing as many visual aids as possible fairly high up on the walls in your room.

Instead of telling students to keep their eyes on their papers during their tests, remind them to look up and see the pictures or mental movies they took when they first learned the material being presented on the test. You will find this very empowering for the students because they will learn to rely on their internal images as they learn and retrieve information during their tests.

> *You will be showing the students how to access visual memory by having them use their eye movements to see a picture in their mind.*

Chapter 1

How Children Learn vs. How Schools Test

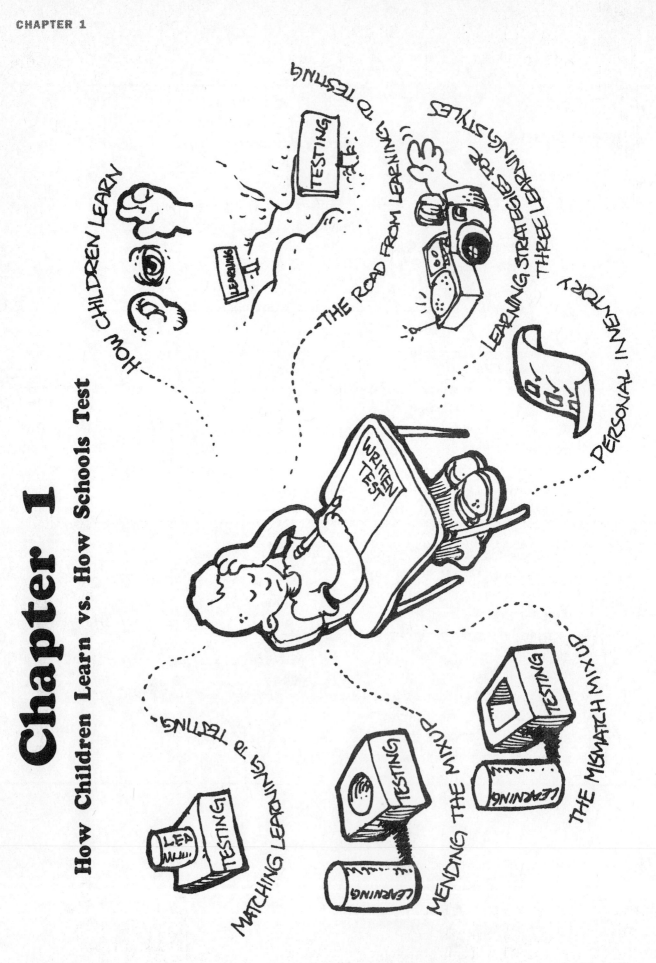

Chapter 2

The Reading Solution~
Foundations First Success Program

In This Chapter

- Can You See It?

- Why 20/20 Eyesight Is Not Good Enough

- LD/ADHD Behavior Look-Alikes

- The Link between Delinquency and Vision Problems

- The Link between Vision and School Success

Can
You See It?

Picture reprinted with permission from OEP Foundation

*C*an you identify this picture in 60 seconds or less?

Questions about the picture will follow. You will be graded on your answers. Your report card will indicate how well you did within the time limit.

Answer these questions about the picture:

1. What is this object?
2. What function does it serve?
3. What can its different colors be?
4. Who is helped by this object?
5. Where does this object live?
6. What other uses does this object have?

This is a familiar subject. You may turn the picture in any direction to figure out what it is.

Need another hint? "Got milk?"

Turn the picture on its side (hold the top right corner of the page and turn it to the right 90 degrees) and you will see the upper body outline of a cow. Notice the black nose at the bottom of the picture, face and ear outline near the top. Seeing the picture helps you have the understanding you need to answer the questions.

Imagine that you were taking a timed test on the picture and had to answer questions on it. How did you feel if you could not recognize it and therefore were not able to answer the questions? If you did not identify the picture in the time allowed, you have failed the test. This is not a test of your intelligence, but of your visual and perceptual skills. Put yourself in the place of a student and imagine that your friends could identify the picture and you could not.

If you did not identify the picture as a cow within the time limit, imagine the frustration you would feel when you received a failing grade. This is the feeling many students with undetected visual problems live with on a daily basis. Steven's story will help explain why.

STEVEN'S STORY

When Steven, a fifth grader, first arrived for his special reading class with me, he seemed very nervous. I watched him carefully and after a few moments, I could see why.

We sat down together and I asked him to read aloud from the book he had brought. I wanted to get a sense of how he felt when he read. He said he didn't want to read and begged to return to his regular classroom teacher.

I told him I knew that reading felt painful for him, but, together, we would change that over the next few weeks. Steven asked how I knew that reading was so uncomfortable for him. I smiled gently and said that sometimes kids see the letters and words on a printed page differently. I said that not all people see them in the same way.

He seemed shocked to find this out. "They don't?" he asked. "No," I said, and picked up a word card and started jumping up and down with it. I said, "See, some kids tell me that the words look like they are jumping all around. And some kids say it looks like there are two of some of the letters running together. Even more say there are no marks at the end of sentences. Sometimes they tell me that they get into trouble because they know a word on one page and not on the next. Then they say that everyone says they are not trying hard enough. Does any of this happen for you?"

Steven looked amazed and said, "Yes. All of it happens, but no one ever asked me about it until now. I thought everybody saw these things but was just smarter than I was. I felt so dumb because I got such bad grades whenever I had to read anything. That's why they said I needed these special reading classes."

Just after Steven told me this, I glanced at his cumulative folder. He had passed the school vision screening with 20/20 eyesight.

> *Twenty-twenty eyesight . . . has little relationship to reading, which occurs at between 11 to 16 inches from the eyes.*

WHY 20/20 EYESIGHT IS NOT GOOD ENOUGH

Look back at the picture at the beginning of the chapter. More than likely you could *see* the picture. But seeing is not the same as *vision*. Vision is the ability to make meaning from what you see.

If you did not identify the picture within the time limit, your failing grade is not a result of low intelligence, a learning disability, ADHD, or not trying hard enough. It is simply a matter of your eyes not interpreting the object well enough to be able to answer the questions. Even though you could clearly see the picture, you may not have been able to put the parts together and make meaning from it. Even though you may have 20/20 eyesight, you still may not have been able to correctly identify the picture as a cow.

> *Both good eyesight and good vision are necessary to be able to read.*

Twenty-twenty eyesight is a result of a test for acuity at a distance of 20 feet. It means that you can see a letter of a certain size from 20 feet away. It has little relationship to reading, which occurs at between 11 to 16 inches from the eyes. The traditional eyesight test result gives no information about what happens when you read or the skills you need to be able to read efficiently.

Both good eyesight and good vision are necessary to be able to read. Reading requires a complex set of visual and brain tasks that occur simultaneously, and eyesight is only one of them. According to the Optometric Educational Foundation, vision involves over 20 visual abilities and more than 65 percent of all the pathways to the brain. This means that perception, comprehension, and memory all depend on the efficiency of an individual's visual system.

Good visual skills are not a matter of chance—they are developed before a child comes to school through a series of experiences during the first few years of life. The degree of vision development will depend upon the quality and quantity of those experiences. When students come to school without adequate and efficient visual skills, they cannot be expected to perform well in reading, writing, copying, or even playing sports. Poorly developed or inadequate visual skills represent the ultimate mismatch between learning and testing, because a student cannot be expected to answer questions on a written test that cannot be deciphered.

Vision is the ability to use the information gained from *sight* and transform it into a useful and meaningful concept. Vision, just like speaking and walking, is a learned skill and must be developed with the proper activities and training.

In Steven's case, although he had passed a school vision screening with 20/20 eyesight, his visual skills were poorly developed. He could not read efficiently and received very poor grades as a result. His poor visual skills affected nearly everything he was asked to do in school and resulted in his being labeled learning disabled.

For the next few weeks, Steven spent about 15 minutes a day doing special vision exercises to strengthen his visual skills. He learned to read easily, for longer periods of time, and without any strain. Steven no longer needed his learning disability label.

As a reading specialist, my experience has been that many who cannot read efficiently and at age-appropriate levels, or cannot sustain their focus for long periods of time, have undetected vision or visual-perceptual problems. If these problems are not diagnosed and treated, both children and adults are at risk for academic failure or worse.

According to Mary Meeker, Ed.D., the founder of the Structure of Intellect (SOI) Systems in Vida, Oregon, poor vision is one of the major health problems in the United States. It goes relatively unnoticed because poor visual skills are demonstrated by a failure to learn to read rather than as poor health. This failure in reading then generalizes to failure in school and increasing illiteracy rates (Meeker 2000).

LD/ADHD BEHAVIOR LOOK-ALIKES

Children who have visual or visual-perceptual problems may display the same symptoms as if they are learning disabled or have attention-deficit hyperactivity disorders. They tend to act out their frustrations in the classroom, appear lazy, unmotivated, and do not earn expected grades.

Parents and teachers often think their children are simply looking for attention or underachieving when the real problem is undetected vision problems. Visual problems contribute to academic underachievement, but the problems don't end there. Some believe there is a direct link between vision problems and juvenile delinquency.

THE LINK BETWEEN DELINQUENCY AND VISION PROBLEMS

To compound our national reading problems, extensive research indicates that poorly developed visual skills are closely correlated with juvenile delinquency. According to the most recent report issued by the National Center on Adult Literacy (Haigler 1994), our nation's literacy levels are well below the standards we have set, and the prison population is full of people who are illiterate or not reading even at functional levels. The center's report on prison literacy states:

- 75–90 percent of juvenile offenders have learning disabilities
- up to 50 percent of adult inmates are functionally illiterate
- up to 90 percent of adult inmates are school dropouts

In the Kempsville Place Group Home in Norfork, Virginia, a residential-care facility, Director Thomas Brett added a vision-screening exam and discovered that 50 percent of the boys had visually related learning problems (Shapiro 1992).

Although it cannot be said that inadequate visual skills are the single cause of all learning-disability labels or juvenile-delinquency problems, the importance of vision on these children's self-esteem and ability to function in the classroom cannot be overlooked. Visual skills should be among the first ones evaluated when students enter school because the visual skill demands are so high.

One additional factor that may reduce a child's ability to perform schoolwork is excessive television watching and computer use. Both can create substantial gaps in vision development stages and create problems both in vision and visual acuity by placing stress on the visual system. Students sitting in front of televisions and computer monitors do not shift their focal length frequently enough, which results in visual acuity problems, the need for glasses to see up close, and poor peripheral vision (Kimple 1997).

THE LINK BETWEEN VISION AND SCHOOL SUCCESS

So much that a child is asked to do in the classroom depends on good visual skills. It has been estimated that 75–90 percent of all classroom learning comes to the students via the visual pathways. If there is any interference with these pathways, the student will probably experience difficulty with learning tasks (Heinke 1981).

Any child may be at risk for visual problems. Due to undetected vision problems, Lucy Johnson-Nugent, daughter of the former president, Lyndon Johnson, nearly dropped out of school while her father was in the White House. She explained her personal learning experiences in a *Family Circle* article (Johnson 1971).

After taking nearly every test imaginable, Lucy was told she was bright but not living up to her potential. She became so frustrated that she began blacking out during her tests. It was only after visiting a local behavioral optometrist and discovering that she had tracking and focusing problems that distorted everything she tried to read or write that Lucy was able regain her confidence and stay in school. After taking a course of vision therapy, Lucy's grades went from Cs and Ds to As and Bs; she became an honor student.

Lucy later became the head of an organization called Volunteers for Vision and helped screen several thousand children for the kinds of visual problems she experienced. She says, "If the key to a better society is education, then the key to a better education is better vision. If you don't have that key, you can't open the door to a better life."

The Facts about Reading Problems

According to the resolution adopted at the National PTA Convention in 1999:

- An estimated 10 million children (ages 0–10) suffer from vision problems.
- When accurately diagnosed, learning-related vision problems can be treated successfully and permanently.

■ Typical vision evaluations/screenings test for only a few of the necessary learning-related visual skills (distance acuity, such as 20/20 eyesight, stereo vision, and muscle balance), leaving most visual skill deficiencies undiagnosed.

■ More comprehensive visual skill tests must be provided in school vision screening programs, to be performed by qualified and trained personnel.

■ Few students, parents, teachers, administrators, or public health officials have knowledge of the relationship between poorly developed visual skills and poor academic performance.

National Reading Proficiency Levels

Reading scores nationwide continue to remain flat, illustrating the need for some deeper investigation into causes and solutions. Inadequate visual skills are heavily correlated with reading problems and failure to achieve.

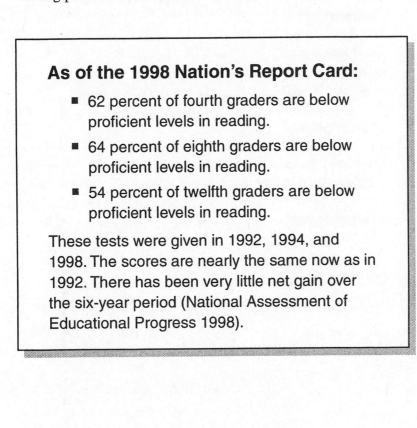

As of the 1998 Nation's Report Card:

- 62 percent of fourth graders are below proficient levels in reading.

- 64 percent of eighth graders are below proficient levels in reading.

- 54 percent of twelfth graders are below proficient levels in reading.

These tests were given in 1992, 1994, and 1998. The scores are nearly the same now as in 1992. There has been very little net gain over the six-year period (National Assessment of Educational Progress 1998).

Tying Performance to Visual Skills

- In Sequoia Union High School, Palo Alto, California, the lowest quartile of all entering ninth graders who were failing in school were tested. All were examined by local developmental optometrists and were found to have subtle vision failure. Every one of these children had been deemed visually proficient on the standard eye exam, and each had spent nine years failing to learn to read (Maxwell 2000).

- In West Los Angeles, optometrists doing volunteer vision screenings through the Lions Club found that 47 percent of children had vision problems. The exams were more comprehensive than simple distance acuity screenings (Fisher 1999).

- In a peer-reviewed journal article relates a phenomenon replicated in hundreds of other studies. In 1996, The New York State Optometric Association Vision Screening Battery (NYSOA) was administered to 81 at-risk elementary, middle, and high school students. The objective was to rule out vision difficulties as contributors to academic problems, such as ADD, ADHD, dyslexia, oppositional-defiant behavior, and so on. Ninety-seven percent of the students with behavioral problems failed at least one of the NYSOA subtests (Johnson et al. 1996).

Research information like this indicates the need to provide adequate school screenings and treatment programs. As a reading specialist, I continue to be concerned that every school may not have an adequate learning-related vision-screening program. Screening and treatment for vision problems will go a long way toward raising students' reading scores and building the strong visual foundation that students need throughout their lives.

Special-education spending might be significantly reduced by not having to label children who cannot read as learning disabled.

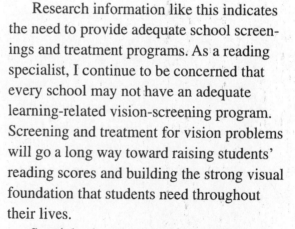

Both students and schools would benefit as priority spending then could shift to helping students master the visual skills needed to be able to read.

I believe that teachers and parents can learn a great deal from the nation's current low reading scores. Although the link between good vision and reading success has been available for many years, one of the primary reasons we haven't achieved our goals in reading is because the proper screening and treatment programs have not been implemented in enough schools.

In the next chapter, you'll discover what teachers and schools can do specifically to raise students' reading scores. Parents can participate, too, by educating themselves about visual skills and their link to reading abilities.

> *Screening and treatment for vision problems will go a long way toward raising student reading scores and building the strong visual foundation that students need throughout their lives.*

Chapter 2
The Reading Solution

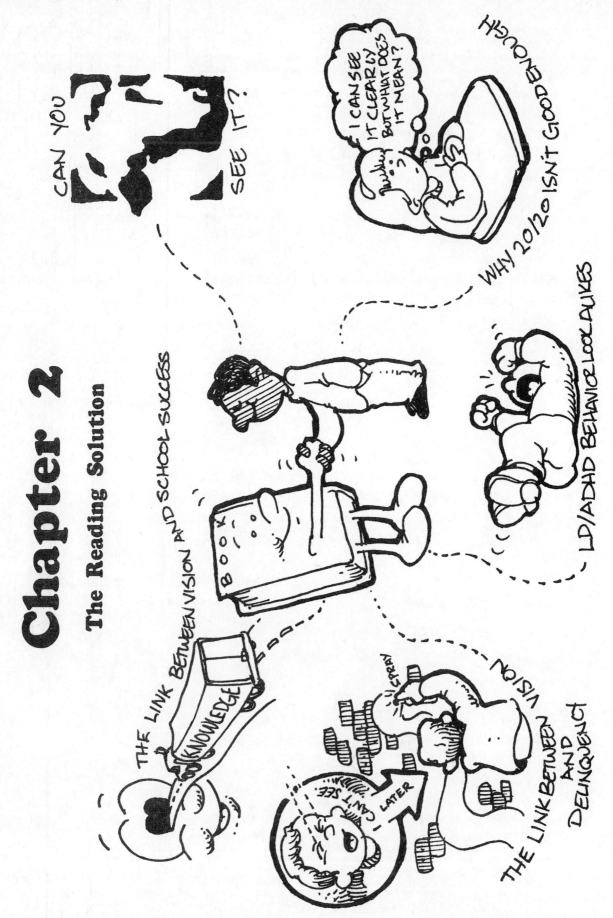

Chapter 3

What You and Your School Can Do to Raise Reading Scores

In This Chapter

- Overview

- Skills Needed for Vision

- Using the Reading Inventory to Assess Visual Skills

- Vision-Training Exercises

- What Teachers Can Do to Reduce Visual Stress

- School Screening and Equipment

- Visual Training Pays Off

Overview

*I*n this chapter you will learn what you can do as a parent or classroom teacher to improve students' visual skills and raise reading scores:

1. Learn about the foundational visual skills needed for reading success (see page 35).

2. Administer the performance-based reading inventory to your students (see page 42).

3. Offer vision-training exercises in the classroom whenever possible (see page 45).

In addition, there are several steps that your school can take to implement a learning related vision-screening program:

1. Implement a learning-related schoolwide vision screening for all students (see page 49). Refer for help when needed.
2. Identify and use recommended resources and exercises to strengthen students' visual skills (see page 134).
3. Teach students to relieve their own visual stress (see page 53).

SKILLS NEEDED FOR VISION

The following is a list of skills needed for academic success.

VISUAL SKILL	EFFECTS ON READING
1. **Visual Acuity**—the ability to see clearly at near and far distances	Students with poor acuity may have difficulty copying from the chalkboard or overhead; will not do well in sports; have trouble with reading and copying from books to paper.
2. **Tracking**—the ability to follow a line of print across the page and to fix the eyes on the appropriate point when finished, then begin following the next line; the ability of the eyes to follow a moving object accurately and smoothly	With poor tracking skills, students may lose their place when reading and read more slowly, often using a marker or their fingers to keep their place.
3. **Eye-Teaming or Binocularity**—the ability to coordinate and align the eyes together; eye alignment at both near and far distances	If this skill is not adequate, students may develop either *exophoria*, which is a tendency for the eyes to deviate outward, or *esophoria*, a tendency for the eyes to deviate inward. Tires easily, covers one eye.
4. **Focusing**—the ability of the eye to adjust the lens power to provide maximum clarity at various distances; looking quickly from near to far and back again without any blurring or discomfort	Students with a focusing problem will have trouble copying from a book, chalkboard, or overhead projector, and may work too close to the paper or the book.
5. **Convergence and Divergence**—the ability of the eyes to turn inward or outward and look at objects close up, then far away, and back again; these skills are closely related to eye-focusing skills; when reading, the eyes must be turned inward toward each other and aimed at the reading task	Weakens the ability to read for longer periods of time; may reduce comprehension. Students with convergence problems may often try to avoid reading or have a short attention span. May lose their place, omit small words, or confuse small words such as *the, that, what*, and so on.
6. **Eye-Hand Coordination or Visual-Motor Integration**—the ability of the vision system to coordinate the information received through the eyes to monitor and direct the hands; essential for handwriting, copying from the board, and in sports	These students often have poor pencil grip, handwriting, and spacing between words, write up or downhill, and have poor posture.
7. **Peripheral Vision**—the ability to fixate on an object and be aware of what is around it at the same time	Poor peripheral vision hinders eye movement from word to word and to the next sentence. Personal safety also involves peripheral vision—for example, bicyclists need good peripheral vision to be aware of oncoming cars.

Additional Visual and Visual-Motor Skills

If the student is visually and perceptually impaired in any way, his or her academic progress may suffer unless the skills are adequately trained. At a minimum, the following skills will determine whether a student is prepared for the demands of the classroom.

■ **Directionality**—an important skill for academic success. In English, we read from left to right, and this visual reflex must be developed. A good measurement of this is to look at the drawing below from Robert H. McKim's *Thinking Visually?* If the visual reflex is from left to right, a duck will be seen. If it is from right to left, a rabbit will be seen. A student must learn to tell left from right to learn to read. All other directions must be learned also. This is a skill that can be easily taught.

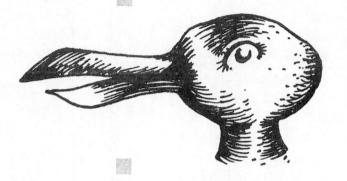

■ **Form Perception**—the ability to see forms clearly and be able to re-create or copy them. Form perception enables a student to discriminate between likenesses and differences. If a student cannot do this accurately, he or she cannot be expected to perceive letters, words, and sentences accurately, let alone make meaning from what is seen. Without this skill a student may reverse letters or words. Form perception can easily be tested by having a student copy the shapes below.

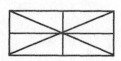

- **Visual Memory**—the ability to recall a visual image. The image may be the symbols that compose the word itself or a picture of what the word depicts. A student will not learn to read or do other classroom work without developing good visual-memory skills.

- **Visualization**—the ability to see things in the mind's eye. Many experts believe that the ability to visualize is closely linked to the ability to think. It is the ability to abstract from specifics. For academic success, this ability is essential. Brain research indicates that memory is more efficient when pictures are created and accessed (see page 16).

- **Figure Ground**—the ability to separate the primary figure from the background. Students who have difficulty doing this will be unable to find words or objects hidden in background patterns; may appear clumsy, bumping into things; and may not be able to sustain reading for longer periods of time due to the visual stress of separating the print from the background on which it appears.

- **Visual Closure**—an interpretive skill that allows a person to quickly identify the difference in similar items and make meaning from them. For example, visual closure is needed to tell the difference between a *C* and an *O*; *that* or *what*, and so on. Students who do not have this ability may see an "o" and think it is a "c."

At a minimum, these skills will determine whether a student is prepared for the demands of the classroom. If the student is visually and perceptually impaired in any way, his or her academic progress may suffer unless the skills are adequately developed.

The chart on page 38 shows how many visual skills are needed to do classroom-related tasks.

If the student is visually and perceptually impaired in any way, his or her academic progress may suffer unless the skills are adequately developed.

Vision Skills Needed for Typical Classroom Tasks

Classroom Tasks	Visual Acuity	Tracking	Eye Teaming—Sustaining Alignment at Near	Eye Teaming—Sustaining Alignment at Far	Focusing—Simultaneous Focusing at Near	Focusing—Simultaneous Focusing at Far	Focusing—Sustaining Focusing at Near	Focusing—Sustaining Focusing at Far	Eye-Hand Coordination & Visual-Motor Integration	Peripheral Vision	Directionality	Form Perception	Visual Memory	Visualization	Figure Ground	Visual Closure
Reading	X	X	X		X		X		X	X	X	X	X	X	X	X
Copying (chalkboard to desk)	X	X		X		X		X	X	X	X	X	X	X	X	X
Copying (at desk)	X	X	X		X		X		X	X	X	X	X	X	X	X
Writing	X	X	X		X		X		X	X	X	X	X	X	X	X
Discussion	X	X	X	X	X	X	X	X		X				X	X	
Demonstration	X	X	X	X	X	X	X	X		X	X	X	X	X	X	
Movies, TV	X	X		X		X		X		X	X	X	X	X	X	
Physical Education, Dancing	X	X	X	X	X	X	X	X	X	X	X	X	X	X	X	
Art, Crafts	X	X	X	X	X	X	X	X	X	X	X	X	X	X	X	X
Play	X	X	X	X	X	X	X	X	X	X	X	X	X	X	X	X
Computers	X	X	X	X	X	X	X	X	X	X	X	X	X	X	X	X
Taking Notes	X	X	X	X	X	X	X	X	X	X	X	X	X	X	X	X

For a student to copy a simple sentence from the chalkboard the following skills are involved:

1. pointing eyes at the chalkboard
2. using figure-ground skills to separate out the material to be copied
3. focusing at a distance
4. coordinating eyes to work together
5. tracking
6. putting the information into visual memory
7. refocusing eyes up close
8. pointing eyes up close
9. using figure ground on the page
10. tracking across the page while writing
11. getting information out of visual memory
12. using eye-hand coordination skills

If a student lacks any one of these skills, his or her work in copying is not at the expected levels. He or she may write uphill, have poor spacing, miscopy, leave out words, and so on.

USING THE READING INVENTORY TO ASSESS VISUAL SKILLS

Those administering the school vision-screening tests often have to deal with large numbers of students at a time. A school nurse, for example, may have to single-handedly screen students at several schools. In these brief screenings, he or she might miss telltale behavior, such as the student covering one eye when reading. This would indicate an eye-teaming problem that needs to be addressed. Teachers and parents are in the best position to pick up visual-stress symptoms, because they observe students over a longer period of time. They listen as students read aloud and observe them performing other classroom tasks; thus they can provide the most accurate observations of a student's visual abilities.

Teachers and parents are in the best position to pick up visual-stress symptoms, because they observe students over a longer period of time.

With the help of the non-profit Optometric Education Program Foundation and the Parents Active for Vision Education (P.A.V.E.) organizations, I have developed a performance-based assessment, which any teacher or parent may use to determine whether a student has undetected visual problems. The following evaluation will enhance the total vision screening for all students. I recommend that a teacher or parent administer this assessment in addition to the school-vision screening. It is called the Wyman Foundational Reading Skills Inventory. A version is included here, or you may download and print this inventory from the website—

http://www.howtolearn.com

WYMAN FOUNDATIONAL READING SKILLS INVENTORY
Directions

Tell the student that you are going to check visual skills they need for reading. Let them know that it is not related to their intelligence, nor is it a graded reading test. Tell the student that certain skills make reading easier, and that sometimes the letters or words on the page may look different to different people. Let students know that you want to know how they feel when they read. Be certain to emphasize the word "feel," as this is one area that is often overlooked when students have difficulty reading.

Select age-appropriate reading material that the student has not read before. Be sure it is not too difficult or too easy. Make a copy for your notes. Before you start, review the types of the students' reading errors on the Wyman Inventory (see page 42). Get familiar with the terms, as you will be making notes about them while the student is reading. Be sure to ask the student if he or she wears glasses for reading. The student should wear them during the screening. Also, record the last time the student had a full eye examination.

Have your student read aloud to you for 10 minutes. Do not shorten this time—it is important to allow the full 10 minutes. If time permits, you can extend this time to 20 minutes. This time will allow for a more accurate performance-based observation. When students experience certain vision problems, they may often start out reading with no discomfort or errors, but become fatigued quickly. Observing them reading aloud for 10 minutes or longer will help determine whether their visual system fatigues after short periods of time. It will also show the specific types of reading errors they are making.

On your copy of the student reading selection, jot down the errors the student makes while reading. Be very specific so you can refer to them later as you mark the types of errors on the inventory checklist. When the student is finished, ask only the starred questions aloud, and make checkmarks next to the questions to which he or she responds *yes*. Then transfer the notes to checkmarks on the appropriate inventory columns. Any checkmarks may indicate problems and make reading more difficult.

After giving the inventory, determine which exercises to do to help correct the types of errors the student made. Set up a training program of from six to eight weeks. Choose from the sample list of vision-training exercises in the next section, or select from the Resources listings (page 134).

Use a weekly progress chart to list activities and results. Do the exercises for about 10 minutes each day. After seven weeks, give the post-test and compare the results with the pre-test.

If, after seven weeks of training, you have not seen the progress desired, it may be necessary to refer the student to an eye doctor for further evaluation. Experts recommend that children have an eye exam once each year to insure proper eye health.

WYMAN FOUNDATIONAL READING SKILLS INVENTORY

- Place checkmarks in boxes next to types of reading problems you observe.
- Use pre-test check boxes during first evaluation and post-test boxes following training exercises.
- Ask students the questions with **. Observe other items as you listen to student read aloud.

Tracking and Eye-Movement Skills

		Pre	Post
** 1.	Do you notice that you accidentally skip some lines or sentences when reading?	❏	❏
** 2.	Do you sometimes lose your place when reading or need to use a marker or your finger to keep your place?	❏	❏
3.	Does the student skip or omit words or letters?	❏	❏
4.	While reading on one line, does the student insert words or letters from the line above or below?	❏	❏
5.	Does the student repeat or reread words?	❏	❏
6.	Is the student's reading slow, choppy, and uneven?	❏	❏
** 7.	Do you find that the longer you read that the reading gets harder for you?	❏	❏
** 8.	If you were given a blank sheet of paper to write on, do you write uphill or downhill?	❏	❏
9.	Does the student leave out small words like *and, the*, and *a* when reading?	❏	❏
** 10.	When playing sports, is it difficult to catch, hit, or throw the ball?	❏	❏

Binocularity or Eye-Teaming Skills

		Pre	Post
** 11.	Do you put your elbow on the table and cover one eye when you read?	❏	❏
12.	If the student writes numbers in a column, do they line up under each other properly?	❏	❏
** 13.	Do you see two of the letters or words on a page or do the words double?	❏	❏
** 14.	Do you tilt your head to one side when you read?	❏	❏
15.	Does the student reverse the order of the letters within words?	❏	❏
** 16.	Do you squint or close one of your eyes when you read?	❏	❏
17.	Does the student leave out letters, phrases, or numbers when reading?	❏	❏

Eye-Hand Coordination Skills

		Pre	Post
** 18.	Do you ever feel like you are clumsy, bump into things, or knock things over?	❏	❏
** 19.	When you write, do you stay on the printed lines or are they hard to see?	❏	❏
** 20.	Do you need to use your hands or fingers to make spacing when you write?	❏	❏
** 21.	Do you have trouble telling your left from your right?	❏	❏

WYMAN FOUNDATIONAL READING SKILLS INVENTORY (CONTINUED)

Visual Form-Perception Skills; Figure Ground; Memory and Motor Skills

	Pre	Post
22. Does the student read the beginning of words and make up his or her own ending?	❑	❑
23. Does the student often read the word *a* as the word *the*?	❑	❑
** 24. Do you have trouble remembering what you just read?	❑	❑
25. Does the student read the endings of words and make up the beginning?		
26. Does the student read the middle of words and make up their own beginning or ending?	❑	❑
27. Does the student reverse letters like *b, d, p, q,* or numbers like 6 and 9, 2 and 5?	❑	❑
28. Does the student confuse similar words like *that* and *what, plus* and *pulse*?	❑	❑
** 29. When you are trying to find hidden figures in drawings is it difficult for you?	❑	❑
** 30. Do you ever feel like you bump into things a lot?	❑	❑

Visual-Form Perception Skills: Laterality, Directionality

	Pre	Post
31. Does the student reverse words like *was* and *saw*?	❑	❑
** 32. Do you know a word on one page and then not recognize it on another?	❑	❑
** 33. Do you move your lips or whisper the words to yourself when you read silently so you can hear the words in your mind?	❑	❑
** 34. When you write or copy, do you reverse letters or words?	❑	❑
** 35. When you want to know the difference between some letters, like *b* and *d*, do you ever draw them or try to figure them out with your fingers?	❑	❑

Refractive Status

Possible farsightedness, nearsightedness, focusing problems (possible eye doctor referral needed)

	Pre	Post
** 36. Do you avoid reading or reading aloud?	❑	❑
** 37. Does reading feel uncomfortable for you?	❑	❑
** 38. Are you restless or easily distracted when you read?	❑	❑
** 39. Do your eyes bother you right now?	❑	❑
** 40. Do your eyes get red and watery?	❑	❑
** 41. Do your eyes hurt, ache, or burn?	❑	❑
** 42. Do your eyes feel dry, sandy, scratchy, or itchy?	❑	❑
** 43. Do you rub your eyes a lot?	❑	❑
** 44. Do you feel tired and drowsy when you read?	❑	❑
** 45. Do you get headaches when you read?	❑	❑
** 46. Do you get nauseous or sick to your stomach when you read?	❑	❑
** 47. Do you open your eyes wide when you read?	❑	❑
** 48. Do you squint or frown when you read?	❑	❑
** 49. Do you blink a lot to try to make the print clearer?	❑	❑
** 50. Do you move closer to the page, or back away when you read?	❑	❑

Pre Post

** 51. Is it an effort to keep looking at the words when you read? ☐ ☐
** 52. Does the print get blurry when you read? ☐ ☐
** 53. Is it ever hard to see the board from where you sit? ☐ ☐
** 54. Do you look away to take frequent breaks? ☐ ☐
55. Does the student's eyes cross or does one eye wander or turn in or out? ☐ ☐

Contrast Sensitivity: Light and Dark

Use colored plastic overlays, available from many office supply stores. Place the overlay directly over the material the student reads. Allow the student to choose the color that makes reading easiest for him or her.

** 56. Do white or glossy pages make reading more difficult for you? ☐ ☐
** 57. Do the words you read seem to get blurry, move around, or change shapes? ☐ ☐
** 58. Do the dots at the tops of the *i*s or the cross mark of the *t*s seem to disappear at times? ☐ ☐
** 59. Do fluorescent lights bother you? ☐ ☐
** 60. Is it harder to read in bright light? ☐ ☐
** 61. Do you miss the punctuation at the end of sentences or does it seem like it is not even there? ☐ ☐
** 62. When you read, does the print seem to blur or become fuzzy or unclear? ☐ ☐
** 63. When you copy from the board to your paper do you notice that you make lots of mistakes? ☐ ☐
** 64. When you copy from another book to your paper, do you seem to make lots of errors? ☐ ☐
** 65. Is it easier to read in dimmer light? ☐ ☐

Skill Retrieval Strategies for Improving Reading Comprehension

** 66. Do you make pictures in your mind of what you have read and then view those pictures again when recalling the material? (*A yes here indicates that the student is making mental images about what was read and then retrieving those images during recall. Students who recall material easily report that they use this visual input, storage, and output method.*)

** 67. When you read, do you say the words to yourself and try to hear the words again when you recall the material? (*A yes here indicates that the student is using an auditory strategy for input and recall of the material. This method may be too slow to allow the student to keep up with large volumes of reading and recall. Visual images form much more rapidly than the spoken word.*)

** 68. When you read, do you mostly have certain feelings about the material and then access those feelings again when trying to recall the material? (*A yes here indicates that the student is using a kinesthetic strategy. Because students recall how they felt about the material and not much actual detail from what was read, this process may lack reliability and lower comprehension. Encourage the student to look up and make a mental movie of the reading.*)

VISION-TRAINING EXERCISES

Following are several exercises that you can do in the class-room or at home to help develop some of the important visual skills needed for reading. The goal is to build the visual-perceptual skills that are basic to the areas of reading, writing, and spelling. All exercises here were created for kindergarteners through adults.

A few cautions: Always use reading materials with clear black text and letters of the appropriate size for the grade (see chart below or on page 46). Use good quality reproductions of all materials—purple dittos, smeared, faded, or broken type stresses the visual system and causes students to struggle to keep the letters in focus and clear. Make certain that the lighting is good in the classroom. Daylight or full-spectrum lighting is best. Fluorescent lighting is the worst choice (Ott 1988).

Exercise I: Visual Discrimination

Objective

To develop visual discrimination, tactile discrimination, and motor coordination

Instructions

First, have the student use templates to trace various geometric shapes. Make sure that the student holds the pencil properly, sits straight, and draws in a clockwise direction. Draw circles, triangles, squares, diamonds, ovals, plus signs, and Xs. Use templates until the student can draw these shapes alone. Once the student can draw them independently, draw a set of the shapes yourself. Then have the student copy them exactly to develop motor coordination and visual perception.

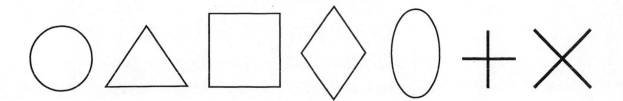

Objective

To develop visual discrimination, motor coordination, left-right orientation, spatial orientation, and sequencing

Instructions

On a piece of paper, draw letters and geometric shapes as seen in the examples below. Put a line after the shapes you want the student to copy. The student will copy each shape to the right of the line. You can increase the difficulty of the task by adding to the number of items to be copied.

b d

p g q

Exercise II: Tracking

Objective

To develop tracking skills needed to follow accurately from line to line

According to Dr. George Spache, creator of the *Diagnostic Reading Scales*, print size should be as follows:	
Grade 1	**14–18-point**
Grades 2–3	**14–16-point type**
Grade 4	12–point type
Grades 5–8	10–12-point type

Instructions

Give the student an article from a book, with letters in the appropriate size for the grade (see point-size chart on facing page). Have the student circle all the letters that you choose, one at a time. For example, select an *e* and have the student place his or her pencil on the first *e* they find, hold the pencil down, circle it in a counter-clockwise direction, and keep the pencil moving on the paper until they find the next *e*. Then have the student circle the next *e* in the same way as the first. Make sure that the pencil stays on the paper on each line and is not lifted until he or she changes lines. This is a sample of what the student may do while looking for the letter *e* throughout the article.

This is a sample of what the child will do while looking for the letter e throughout the article.

Objective

To develop tracking, focusing, and convergence skills

Instructions

Hang a ball from the ceiling (use a hook and string). Swing the ball from side to side and have the student follow the ball without moving his or her head. To increase the difficulty level, place letters on the ball and have the student call out the letters as you swing the ball toward him or her.

WHAT TEACHERS CAN DO
TO REDUCE VISUAL STRESS

The following chart offers solutions to classroom visual stress.

PROBLEMS OBSERVED	SUGGESTED SOLUTIONS
difficulty copying from book	▪ Have another student help using carbon paper. ▪ Reduce number of items (only copy odd or even numbers).
difficulty copying from board	▪ Make letters larger with more space between them. ▪ Put same material on paper for student to copy.
loses place while reading	▪ Allow student to use marker. ▪ Suggest that student look away from book for 30–60 seconds to relax eyes. ▪ Have the student trace the figure in the air, first with one hand and then the other to activate both brain hemispheres and integrate all visual fields.
numbers do not line up when copying or creating math	▪ Use large graph paper. ▪ Make each number with a separate color.
misses punctuation, omits words, complains that words jump around, cannot read for prolonged periods	▪ Use colored overlays. Place one color at a time over the printed page. Allow student to tell you which color makes reading easier.

Refer students for appropriate help when you observe them holding their books too closely, covering one eye as they work, rubbing their eyes, being unable to sustain reading focus for normal periods of time, or complaining about blurry print. These students may have refractive problems and need glasses to improve their eyesight.

While screening goes a long way toward preventing problems and pinpointing symptoms, it cannot treat problems such as the need for glasses or training to correct crossed eyes. When serious problems surface as a result of school-vision screenings and performance-based observations, the services of an eye doctor will be needed.

SCHOOL SCREENING AND EQUIPMENT

Schoolwork clearly places a heavy demand upon a student's visual system. The student's visual system must function at optimum levels if students are to learn to read efficiently.

The human visual system did not evolve with today's visual demands in mind. Sustained computer use, small print, longer books, and prolonged periods of television watching place stressful demands on the visual system that many students (and adults) are unprepared to meet. Further, reading is more than just another subject—it is the gateway into the entire curriculum. Therefore, efforts to raise reading scores will be hampered without the proper visual-skills screening and follow-up treatment if needed.

> *Sustained computer use, small print, longer books, and prolonged periods of television watching place stressful demands on the visual system that many students (and adults) are unprepared to meet.*

When students enter school they are usually given a vision screening that nearly always includes the Snellen Eye Test (basic wall chart). If this is the only test given, most visual problems will go unrecognized. The Snellen Eye Test has no relationship to reading at near point. It was developed in the 1860s to test students' ability to see the chalkboard from the back of the room. Students stand at a distance of 20 feet from the chart, cover one eye at a time, and are asked if they can see letters of a certain size. This typical school vision screening is not fully learning-related, as it tests only eyesight, not vision.

I have often observed students waiting in line for the Snellen screening quickly trying to memorize the chart before it is their turn. Even if a student receives a legitimate score of

20/20 eyesight, reading problems may still arise.

Uninformed parents or teachers may assume that a 20/20 vision report means the student has good eyesight and can read. If the student has trouble reading, both parents and teachers may conclude the student is not trying hard enough. This erroneous conclusion may result in the student being incorrectly labeled as an underachiever. A good school-vision screening will eliminate this problem and adequately inform both teachers and parents of the student's visual abilities.

The Effects of Vision on Learning and School Performance

In setting up school-vision screenings, teachers, parents, students, and student-study teams are often involved. Many aspects of the learning process must be considered, from behavioral to environmental concerns. Since so much of classroom learning comes to the student via visual pathways, effective vision screenings must be learning-related. This means they must include both eyesight and vision. The following section gives recommendations for school vision screenings.

Doctor Screenings, Equipment Screenings, and Performance-Based Evaluations

The best option for successful school screenings is to have behavioral optometrists screen all students. They are specially trained to perform learning-related screenings, and will be able to spot quickly those students who will need further help to strengthen their visual skills.

In many areas, optometrists will do vision screenings at no charge, and some districts will pay minimal fees out of district funds. A list of doctors qualified to do these screenings can be found at the websites of these organizations: Optometric

Education Program (OEP), College of Optometrists in Vision Development (COVD), and Parents Active for Vision Education (P.A.V.E). (See Resource listings, page 134.)

To cover the cost of optometry services, some school systems have successfully procured grants. Others look to a variety of school, state, or federal funding sources.

Your school may choose instead to purchase special equipment in order to do its own vision screenings. This equipment will give better information than the standard distance test, such as the Snellen Chart. Schools should consult with a qualified eye doctor before purchasing and/or using this screening equipment.

> *The best option for successful school screenings is to have behavioral optometrists screen all students.*

My recommendations for the best pieces of equipment to select and the skills they measure are as follows:

1. The *New York State Optometric Association Vision Screening Battery (NYSOA)* is the product of a seven-year combined effort of optometrists who specialize in pediatric vision and vision training, a reading and curriculum specialist, a school psychologist, and a statistician. Their goal was to develop a battery of tests that could screen a student's visual needs as they apply to today's classroom environment. Although the tests cannot replace the examination typically performed in the doctor's office, they identify students with vision problems that will affect their academic performance. The NYSOA contains the following tests and is an inexpensive way to measure several vision needs:

   ■ acuity at near and far; muscle coordination; visual-motor integration; eye-tracking skills, convergence ability; color deficiency; sensory-motor coordination; fusion; stereopsis; phorias (near and far); myopia; hyperopia; high astigmatism; lazy eye; binocularity; and eye-hand coordination

2. The *Keystone Telebinocular* is commonly used to provide information on visual acuity (clarity) at both near and far distances; depth perception; and binocularity (two-eyed coordination). It will not, however, identify problems with focusing skills, visual perception, or eye-tracking movements.

3. The *Titmus 2a* vision screener provides some useful information in only five minutes. It can evaluate far, near, and peripheral vision; color perception; muscle balance; depth perception; and binocularity. It will not measure all the visual skills necessary for school success.

Don't sacrifice time for quality when considering equipment to use. Although some screenings make take only five minutes, they will not necessarily evaluate the skills students need to perform classroom tasks.

VISUAL TRAINING PAYS OFF

Since vision is a learned skill, it is easily taught and students can improve their reading, writing, and even athletic abilities in just a few weeks. The training will fill in gaps they missed in early childhood.

Liz Langer, a special-education teacher at Lincoln Elementary School in Owatonna, Minnesota, regularly works with students who need vision training help to become better readers. Ms. Langer said, "I had one student who I had worked with, one-on-one, for three and a half years. As a fourth grader, this student still read at pre-primer level. After fourth grade, he took vision therapy training over the summer. When he returned to school, we retested him. His reading level had increased over *three* years! It was like a miracle...as I worked with him, he almost taught himself to read. Now, whenever parents have students with reading problems and ask what else they can do, we let them know that vision training is available. In fact, a behavioral optometrist in our state conducts vision screenings at no charge."

Many professional sports teams use vision training as a competitive edge, according to an article that appeared in the OEP's *Sports Vision* in 1998. Vision training helped the 1984 U.S. women's and men's volleyball teams win bronze and gold medals. In addition, professional teams like the New York Yankees, Kansas City Royals, Dallas Cowboys, and Chicago Black Hawks have all learned that vision training keeps their visual skills at optimal levels. The article also said that many airline pilots take vision training to improve the quality of their performance.

> *Now, whenever parents have students with reading problems and ask what else they can do, we let them know that vision training is available.*

Although vision training in a doctor's office is the preferred training method, many schools and parents may not be able to afford it. Rather than leave a student's visual needs unattended, there are excellent programs that can be implemented inexpensively at school and at home. I know of many schools that have been able to add vision training onsite at minimal cost. Students can do these exercises for just 10 to 15 minutes per day for about six to seven weeks and achieve remarkable gains in their reading ability.

Tips for Helping Students Reduce Visual Stress

1. Suggest that students hold their book at a 45-degree angle when reading. Laying the books flat on the desk stresses the visual system due to the way the light hits the retina.

2. Encourage students to take frequent breaks when working at the computer. Have them stand up, look far away, and then close up again.

3. Consider slanted desks or slat boards for the students. These have the best angle for posture, reduce neck stress, and encourage better visual skills when reading and writing.

4. Encourage proper pencil grip (use plastic grip holders) and proper posture to reduce arm, neck, and shoulder strain.

Chapter 3

What You and Your School Can Do to Raise Reading Scores

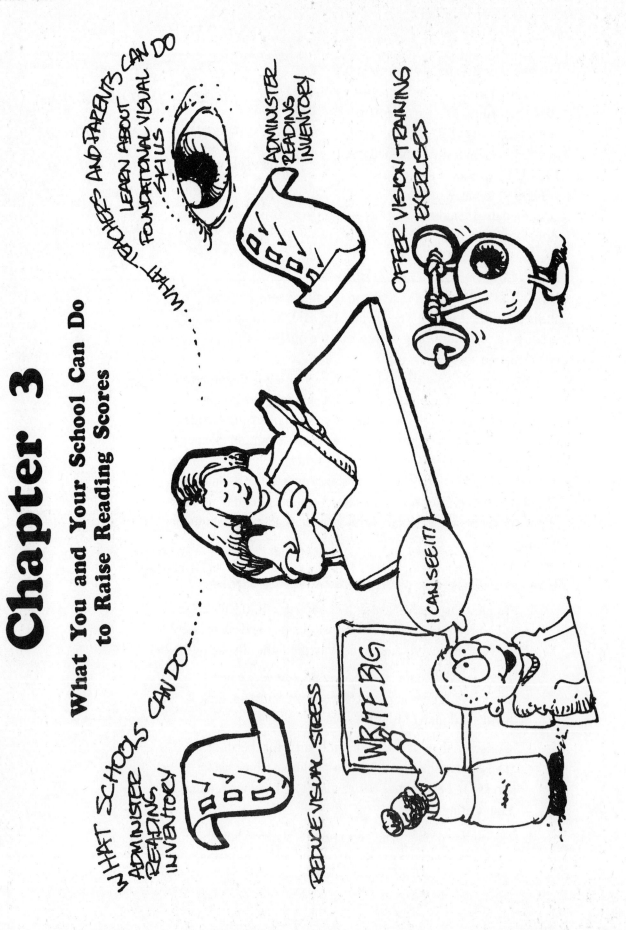

Chapter 4
Word Wizard Vocabulary Mastery

In This Chapter

- **Recipe for Vocabulary Success**

- **Mnemonics Strategy for Vocabulary Success**

Recipe
for Vocabulary
Success

*E*very subject has new vocabulary that students must learn. Some students may feel as if they almost need to master new foreign languages as they move through their day in different subject areas.

Students who can master new words and their meanings naturally use a particular process, which can be easily taught to other students. I have used this process successfully for many years with teachers, K–12 students, and medical students. I believe that everyone is able to make the connections and pictures needed to become a "word wizard."

Your students will be using multimodal (visual, auditory, kines-thetic) input channels (Hart 1991) as they learn this brain-compatible vocabulary strategy, but they will depend primarily on the visual portion of the strategy for recall during written tests. The power of memory is multiplied many times when we connect an association to the picture. An association is simply something that is connected to and re-minds us of something else; for example, the word *Romeo* elicits *Juliet*; *Batman* conjures up *Robin* (Sousa 1995).

Perhaps you have a favorite song that reminds you of a special time in your life. The feeling that you get every time you hear the song is called an association. In other words, you connect a certain set of feelings to a picture of the event when you hear the song. To illustrate this point in one of my educa-tion classes, I played Whitney Houston's version of *The Greatest Love of All*. A teacher immediately smiled and told me that this song was played at her wedding. She saw herself walking down the aisle and had very good feelings as she listened to the song.

> *Perhaps you have a favorite song that reminds you of a special time in your life . . . you connect a certain set of feelings to a picture of the event when you hear the song.*

Word Wizard Vocabulary Strategy

Objective

By using the picture-association technique, successful students are easily able to access words and their meanings. The way they do this is to look up and see a picture of the word in their mind along with the connected meaning.

Materials

- large unlined colored notecards, or half-sheets of various colored construction paper
- crayons or markers

Preparation

To insure success, have the student choose three to five new words to learn and then follow the example below. If the student is younger, you may only want to select one word to learn. Review the visual eye-brain strategy you learned in chapter 1 (see page 18) before beginning the word wizard vocabulary strategy. This will be used to reinforce the visual memory strategy used to recall words and their meanings during the student's written tests.

Instructions

Have the students look at the word(s) to be learned. Tell them first to make an association or connection with that word. It is very important that students create this connection first. In order to make an association, have the students ask themselves: "What does the sound of this word remind me of?"

What does this remind me of?

To illustrate this exercise, we will use this example: When learning the Portuguese word *noz* during language class, ask the students what the sound brings to mind. A student might say it reminds him or her of *nose*. (This procedure is the same for English words and their definitions, and even works with conceptual, words of all parts of speech—nouns, verbs, adjectives, and so on.)

When first making this association, tell the students not to think of the actual meaning of the word *noz* at this time; they are only to think of the sound it brought to mind. Once a connection is made, then they are ready to connect it to a picture of what the word actually means.

Now have students think of the actual meaning of the word *noz*: *walnut*. Next, tell them to create a picture of their association (nose) with a walnut in a single image in their mind. Add humor to this, which will strengthen their memory of the word *noz*. In the example, I created a picture of a nose shaped like a walnut.

Tell the students to draw a picture of their association connected to the actual meaning of the word. Use colored medium-tip markers and place this image in the center of the card. Remember, all the students are doing here is connecting two images: the association and the actual picture of the meaning of the word. Make certain the students include as much color as possible, as it serves to enhance memory. Now have the students write the word (*noz*) just below the picture in the center. Use only one color for the word *noz*.

In another color, write a short definition of the word in either the upper left or upper right hand corner of the card, depending on where the student looks for visual memory (see chapter 1, page 18).

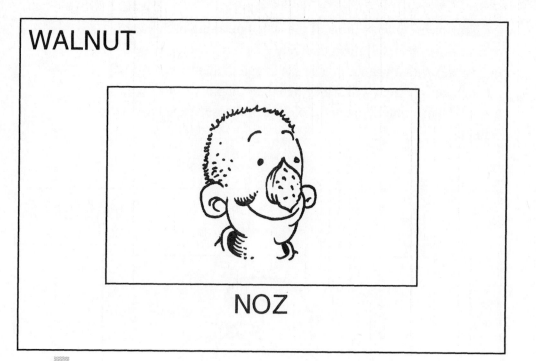

WALNUT

NOZ

To strengthen the memory process you will want to add music as the students draw their pictures. (See Resources listing, page 135, for recommended music.) While playing this music, have each student hold the card above eye level (up to the left or up to the right visual memory position) and say the word and then the definition aloud. For this example, they will say *noz—walnut.* Repeat this process of holding up the card and saying the word and definition twice. If your students are younger, you may want to repeat the exercise three or more times. Tell your class to say *noz—walnut* loudly; then repeat it softly. Then tell your students to take a picture of the word and its meaning as they says it aloud again.

Repeat the process above until your students have made word cards with associations and pictures of as many words as you determine appropriate for their age level. Remember to start out with fewer words as you introduce the technique so that all students are assured of success. *Note:* Students must hold the cards up and above their eye level. Holding them lower is associated with learning styles other than visual.

Have all of the students close their eyes. Test them aloud by asking either the definition or the word. Have them raise their hands high if they know the answer. This will check for

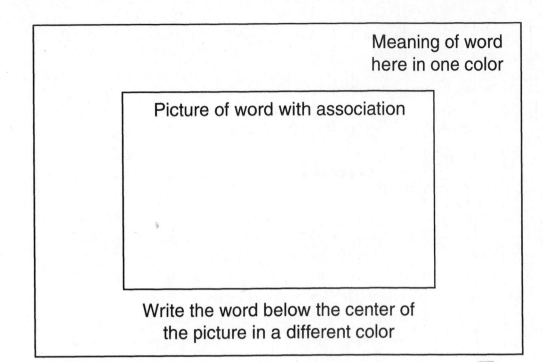

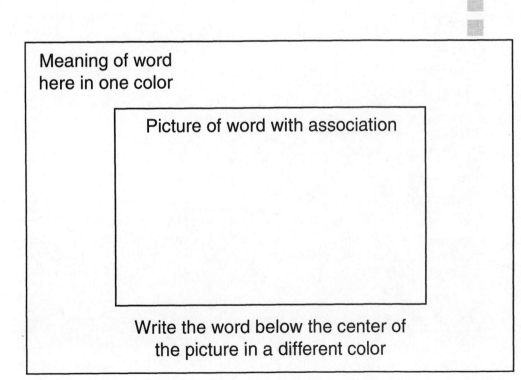

Ask all your students to sit as if they are totally successful and then give the written test prepared for them.

knowledge, and protect the students from any embarrassment if they do not know. If a student does not raise his or her hand, have the whole class look at their word card again for review.

Now, tell the students you will be testing them in writing on the meanings of the new words learned. Ask them if they now have a visual-memory strategy to use to remember the word during the test. Remind them to rely on this strategy during the test.

Tell students to *"assume your success position!"* Ask all your students to sit as if they are totally successful and then give the written test prepared for them. Try it yourself now. Sit as if you are totally successful. Notice the change in your posture and breathing. Put posters around your room modeling the success position. Take pictures of various students in their success position and put them up. Before a test or when learning something new, have all your students sit in their success position. *Expect success!*

Teacher Kim Whichard, in Livermore, California, says this about the success position:

"I was totally amazed at the difference those two words made, not only the students' posture but in their attitude and work as well. It wasn't long before they were reminding each other of the success position. A positive, energetic 'I-can' spirit awakened my students when those two simple words were used."

Testing Success Hints

■ Remind your student to look up to their left or up to their right for visual memory during tests. It is always a good idea to mix the questions so that you are asking for some words and some definitions. That way students will continue to rely on their visual pictures during recall.

■ If the students study at home for the test, make certain to tell them not to study the words aloud if you are giving a written test. They need to match the way they study with the way in which they will be tested.

■ Before the test, have the students sit as if they are totally successful. Remind them to look onto their vocabulary screen in their mind and see the pictures they drew on the cards.

MNEMONICS STRATEGY FOR VOCABULARY SUCCESS

Mnemonics is another excellent strategy for helping students learn their new words. This can be either an auditory or visual technique. Again, make sure the students learn to rely on the visual portion of the strategy for effective memory during tests.

Mnemonics is any technique that improves the efficiency of the memory. There are countless mnemonic techniques available and many students have used the following strategy with great success.

As in the previous example, you will want your students to create a word card for the word and mnemonic and hold it in their visual-memory position as they study. Once they create the mnemonic, have them use the procedure to study what they are learning.

To illustrate this exercise, here is a picture, with its mnemonic example, that I use to help first-year medical students memorize the bones in the hand:

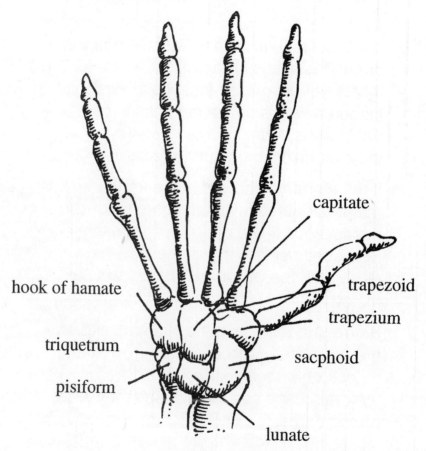

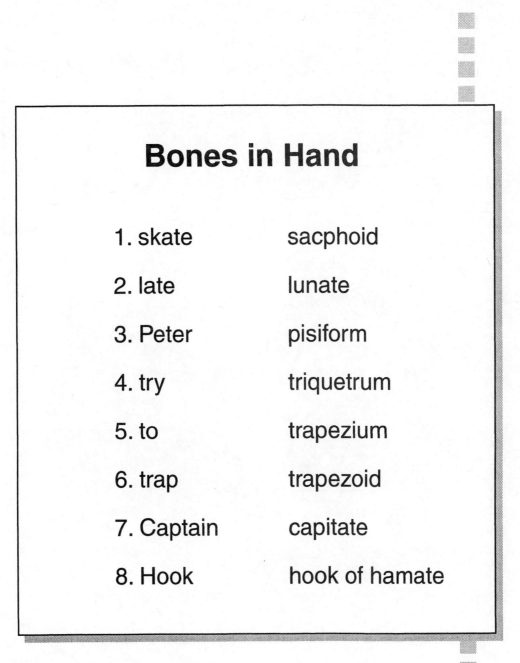

Bones in Hand

1. skate   sacphoid

2. late   lunate

3. Peter   pisiform

4. try   triquetrum

5. to   trapezium

6. trap   trapezoid

7. Captain   capitate

8. Hook   hook of hamate

Chapter 4

Word Wizard Vocabulary Mastery

Chapter 5
Recipe for Super Spellers

In This Chapter

- **Jamie's Story**

- **Super Speller Strategy**

- **Spelling Success Hints**

Jamie's *Story*

Jamie is a sixth-grade student who studies her spelling words every week. She writes them down 10 times each and uses them in sentences. The night before the test she practices them out loud with her mom and reviews the words aloud just before the test. On Friday, she takes her test. Jamie is discouraged when her spelling test is returned—another C–. She wonders how much longer this will go on.

Like many students, Jamie has a technique she uses for studying spelling, but it doesn't get the results she wants.

Spelling success means more than just a grade to a student. Students often compare themselves to others in the class and gauge their own self-image by their grades. Spelling appears to be such a simple thing to many teachers and adults; yet, a student who experiences mediocre grades or failure week after week begins to see him or herself as inadequate or worse. Learning is no longer a delight, and the student suffers terribly inside. He or she may even display undesirable behavior as a result of poor spelling grades. Other grades may decline as well.

In order for students to learn to feel successful, they must naturally experience success. The Super Speller Strategy offers a specific strategy that may simultaneously improve self-esteem.

The secret to spelling success is to have a mental image of the word. If you have this picture to rely on, it matches the way you are being tested. If you have ever written a word and then said, "That doesn't look right," you know that you are comparing a mental image of the word with the one you've written.

> *The Super Speller Strategy offers a specific strategy that may simultaneously improve self-esteem.*

Cathy Heissler, a special-education teacher and owner of the Learning for Tomorrow Center in Normal, Illinois, said,

"The Super Speller Strategy changes my students' lives. All of my students went from failing to getting As and Bs. Their self-esteem improves so much that they do better in all their other subjects too!"

Spelling is primarily a visual skill. When students make, store, and recall these images in their mind, their grades increase almost immediately. Even though students may write the words over and over, they may fail to take a mental snapshot of the words they are writing. They are feeling their hands move, but have not created the mental image of each word. Even if they practice their words aloud, without that mental snapshot, they will not get the results they want.

> *Even though students may write the words over and over, they may fail to take a mental snapshot of the words they are writing.*

A teacher who took one of my courses recalled, "I would write my words over and over and just draw a blank during the test. I had nothing to rely on except the feeling of writing them over and over. Once I learned how to take a mental snapshot of the word, I got an A every week."

At this point, you may be saying that you learned to sound words out or learned to spell using phonics. While you may have used your knowledge of phonics to support a visual strategy, phonics alone may not yield good spelling results. If this were the case, districts using phonics-based programs would see excellent results with all their students. Unfortunately, a large percentage of words in the English language are not sound-based.

Unless a person adds a visually based method to check the accuracy of a word, the inconsistencies and rule changes in a phonetic approach can be overwhelming and unreliable.

Super Speller Strategy

Objective

The following is a procedure for teaching the visual spelling strategy. While both auditory and kinesthetic strategies are also used, the key to spelling success is to have the student rely on the visual, mental image they make of the word. This strategy may be easily adapted to whatever spelling program your school uses.

Materials

- ▶ strips of colored paper about 3 inches high and 8 1/2 inches long (you may also use colored notecards)
- ▶ medium-tipped colored markers (crayons will also work but tend to be too thick)
- ▶ overhead projector if available

Preparation

Before beginning the Super Speller Strategy, review the visual eye-brain connection strategy in chapter 1 (page 18). This will help you establish where each student looks up to when remembering a picture. You will use this location, either up to the left or up to the right, as you teach the spelling strategy.

Instructions

To demonstrate this technique to your class, select a student who has a history of difficulty in spelling. (These students will pick up this strategy quickly and enjoy the surprise and admiration of their classmates.) Bring this student to the front of the room and seat him or her comfortably across from you.

Ask the student's favorite color. Have him or her print the word to be learned in that color on the notecard or colored paper. Notice any letter or combination of letters that might need special emphasis. Examples include the *ei* in receive, or *cc* in success. Have the student decorate those letters uniquely in another color; for example, drawing a heart in place of the dot on the *i*.

Have the student think of someone who always makes As in spelling. Ask what would happen to his or her spelling grades if he or she knew the recipe of a person who gets those good grades. The reply will be something along the order of "my spelling grades would go up too."

SUPER SPELLER
STRATEGY SUMMARY

1. Print the word on the colored card, using different colored markers to emphasize unique letters that do not sound as they are spelled.

2. Hold the card up in the visual memory location—up to the left or up to the right.

3. Trace letters with finger while saying word aloud.

4. Notice any letter shapes that are unique. Look at letters above and below the line.

5. Take a mental snapshot of the word—place it on the spelling channel on your magic spelling screen.

6. Write the word down on your paper. Look up and remember how it looked on the spelling screen.

7. Compare what you wrote down with the word card.

8. ***Expect Success!***

Learning vs. Testing ©2001, Zephyr Press

Explain to the student that everyone has a "magic" spelling screen, movie, or TV screen in the mind, and he or she can put their spelling words on it, just as their classmate who is a super speller does. He or she could even "mentally beam the word onto the blackboard in the classroom."

Tell the student that the word is in his or her mind's eye. Show the student exactly where he or she looks up to when recalling a previously seen picture. This is his or her personal visual-memory location. Make sure the student understands that it is up and to his or her left or right. I touch my students on the appropriate shoulder to show them which side, rather than use the words right or left to avoid left/right confusion.

I usually mention to the student that he or she can "tune into" the spelling channel on his or her TV screen anytime he or she wants to remember the words for their test or during writing assignments.

This next step is a variation of the *look, say, cover, write* method used in education for many years. Have the student hold the word card up in his or her visual memory location (above his/her eyes and up to the left or right side). Make sure that the distance is comfortable for the student. If the student wears bifocals or progressive lenses, you want to make sure the location you are holding the card is easy for him or her to see.

Holding the word card in the visual-memory position, have the student trace the letters of the word with his or her index finger. This will give the student a kinesthetic feel for the word while keeping his or head head raised. (This is a strategy from the Slingerland reading method [1996] I have used very successfully with dyslexic students.)

Have the student say the word aloud (auditory strategy). Then ask the student to trace the word with a pencil without actually writing the letters, while the card is still in the air. Notice that you are incorporating the kinesthetic or body-learning style, at the same time you are asking students to rely on the visual learning strategy.

Now, ask the student if there are any interesting combinations of letters, such as the ones he or she may have decorated. Perhaps the student drew a happy face in an *o*. Have him or her say the letter or letters out loud. This gives more time to "focus" visually on the word.

At this point, you may also want to project the word onto the overhead projector. Make the word look just like the student has drawn on the card. Have the class look up and *see* the word on the screen.

Allow the student to notice letter shapes and tell you whether there are any parts of any letters above or below the rest of the letters in the word. For example, the tall part of the *t* and the *h* will go above; *g* and *y* will go below the line. (This is another excellent visual-shape discrimination strategy, long used in spelling and reading instruction.)

Ask the student, "Are there any letters next to each other which are the same?" (For example, double consonants.)

Finally, have the student pretend to snap a mental picture of the word in their mind and store it on his or her visual memory screen (for younger students I call it a "magic spelling screen"). You may flash the word onto the overhead screen or whiteboard if you have one. Take the word card away and remind the student to actually look back to his or her visual memory screen location. Ask the student to remember how the word looked and write the word down.

Expect success! Compare the word the student has written down with the actual word on the card. If you see that it is done correctly, ask the student if he or she would "bet" you a homework pass or recess time that it's correct. You will be able to tell by the way the student answers whether he or she has relied on his or her visual memory and how confident the student feels. When the student says *yes*, that he or she is *sure* it is correct, then hold their card and the word he or she wrote down correctly up for the whole class to see. Make certain everyone applauds. Remember, this is the first time this student has received such accolades. Imagine how wonderful he or she will feel.

Expect Success!

If the word is written down incorrectly, say nothing except, "Let's decorate these letters." Then have them decorate any missed letters in other colors with new drawings. Then, repeat the steps above.

Next, have the student sit in his or her chair facing the class. Stand behind him or her holding the word card up for the class to see. Ask the student to look up into her/his visual memory position and hold your hand up to that location. Ask the student to tell you the last letter of the word. (Never use the actual words "spell the word backwards.") Then, marking the word in the air with your hand, ask for the second to the last letter, the next to last, the next, and finally the first letter of the word. When this is done correctly, reward the student and ask the student to spell the word forward. Do not leave the word in the visual memory screen in a backwards mode.

Ask the student if he/she now has a strategy for recalling spelling words. Have him/her teach the strategy to another student to check for knowledge. (This is great for cooperative learning!) The student should practice with you or other students for two to three weeks. Make certain that you condition your students for success.

Always prepare your student for spelling tests or writing assignments, by telling him/her to "sit as if you are totally successful." Keep encouraging your students to look into their visual-memory screen throughout their tests and during writing assignments. You now have taught them a strategy that they can use quickly and easily in all of their subjects, not just spelling. You have taught them the **how** *of learning far beyond any content you may have introduced. This is how a student becomes a visual learner in the visual world we call school.*

SPELLING SUCCESS HINTS

1. Insure student success and build confidence by introducing the spelling strategy with shorter words. When you do introduce longer words, fold the word card in half and do the process with half the word at a time. Or, ask the student where he or she wants to divide the word.

2. Shorten spelling test lists until the students are totally confident in their new abilities. Make absolutely certain that each time the students study spelling lessons they use the visual memory strategy.

3. Send notes or newsletters home encouraging parents to use this strategy as well. Get them to follow up. Remind parents that testing the student aloud will not match the way they will be tested in the class.

4. Enjoy your success and watch all your students become *super spellers!*

Chapter 5
Recipe for Super Spellers

Chapter 6
Math Facts Mastery

In This Chapter

- How to Master Addition, Subtraction, Multiplication, and Division in Half the Time

- VAK Strategy for Math Facts

- Mental-Imagery Exercises

How
to Master

in Half the Time

What if your students could learn their addition, subtraction, multiplication, and division facts in half the time it usually takes? How would your life be different? Imagine how your students would feel when they passed their math-facts tests with flying colors. Picture yourself moving onto other math concepts more quickly since you've spent less time teaching the facts.

The Math Facts Mastery strategy will help every child in your classroom—even those students you have wondered about who study their math facts exhaustively, yet never quite know them for their tests. It will also help those students who have used flash cards repeatedly and still do not recall their facts during the test.

The students who seem to have given up on learning their math facts are not aware that there are effective strategies available to them. They have struggled only because they have used a learning-style method that does not work well for this type of task.

Several brain studies, done as long ago as the early 1980s, indicate that if children use visual strategies when solving arithmetic problems, they score higher than those who don't. Those who use spatial visualization, visual-motor sequencing, and/or vocabulary/logical/sequential processing during calculation problems were better performers.

> *The students who seem to have given up on learning their math facts are not aware that there are effective strategies available to them.*

This means that students who understand that math is a visual, logical task will be more efficient in their learning and problem-solving abilities. Their thought processes will activate many areas of the brain. They will "see" the facts in their mind rather than relying on just hearing, or using kinesthetic methods such as finger counting.

The following are two strategies that incorporate visual, auditory, and kinesthetic learning strategies. Your students will use each modality as they learn, but will again rely on their visual picture of the facts for more efficient access and recall during their written tests.

Addition and Subtraction

Objective

With the following strategy, your students will be learning addition and subtraction simultaneously, which will decrease their learning time by half. Multiplication and division will be learned simultaneously as well. You can do this strategy by bringing one student to the front of the room to demonstrate, or have all the students do the process at their desks. Directions for the whole-class method follow—adapt accordingly.

Instructions

While playing the music recommended in the Resources listing (page 135), or other music you have chosen, have the students draw a large triangle with colored markers on unlined colored paper. Use as many colored sheets as possible for the different facts. Younger students may use a template you have made.

Instruct students to place the numbers to be added on the outside sides of the bottom of the triangle as you see in the example below. Put a plus sign at the bottom inside of the triangle. Place the answer at the outside edge on the top of the triangle. Draw a minus sign in the inside at top of the triangle.

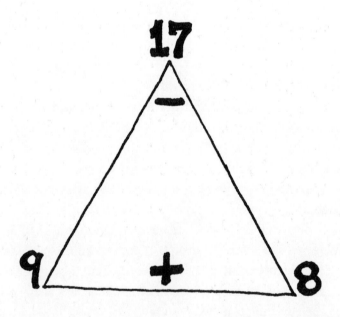

Tell students that they will learn this fact over the next two days. On the first day, tell the students that they do not have to learn the fact today. This takes the pressure away from the thought of immediate mastery. On the second day, tell them that today they will learn the fact. That way, they are already familiar with the fact.

Students hold their triangles up above eye level and in their upper right or upper left visual-memory position. You might call this their magic math screen, or have them tune their TV screen into their math channel.

Ask if they would like to learn the exact strategy used by those students who have an easy time with math facts. Explain that kids who have an easy time see the math facts in pictures, just as if they are seeing a movie screen in their mind. Remind them that they have a movie or magic math facts screen too. This screen is either up to their left or up to their right. Check to make sure that each student knows where his or her own screen is located.

As they are holding the fact in their visual memory position, have the children look at the fact while you say 9 + 8 is _____ and have them fill in the answer aloud.

Then reverse the order, saying 8 + 9 is _____ and have them say the answer aloud. Then say 17 − 9 is _____ and 17 − 8 is _____.

Tell them to trace each of the numbers while you are still holding the card.

As they trace the numbers, they will also say the fact aloud in the various ways it can be presented. Have a lot of fun with this part, as it will help each student get the feel of the fact while relying on the picture.

Explain to students that their eyes are actually like a video camera. They can remember all their facts by looking up to the same picture memory location where they have studied them. Tell them to snap a picture of the fact. Then take the triangle away.

> *Explain to students that their eyes are actually like a video camera. They can remember all their facts by looking up to the same picture memory location where they have studied them.*

Have students draw the triangle in the air with their fingers and say the fact aloud just as before:

9 + 8   is   _____

8 + 9   is   _____

17 − 9   is   _____

17 − 8   is   _____

Let the students know they will be taking a written test on all the forms of this fact. Remind them to look at their magic math screen to get their answers before writing their answers down.

Have students compare what they have written with what is on their triangle. If you notice that any answers are incorrect, have them decorate their triangle with a fun drawing and practice the fact again. If everyone has answered all the questions correctly, it can be extremely effective for them to reward themselves kinesthetically. Tell them to clap or pat themselves on the back as you say "good job."

Multiplication and Division

Objective

The multiplication and division process is virtually the same as the addition and subtraction strategy above. However, you will be making a triangle of a different shape so the child can distinguish between the operations. Use the inverted triangle below and follow the same procedure as for addition and subtraction.

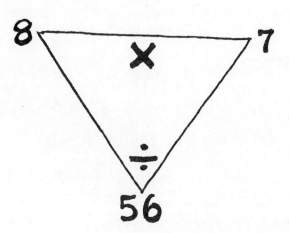

VAK STRATEGY FOR MATH FACTS

For learning multiplication facts, this visual, auditory, and kinesthetic (VAK) strategy relies on visual retrieval of those facts during the test. Joy Ridenour, teacher and director of The Center for Learning and Teaching in Long Beach, California, has created a wonderful book with audiotapes called, *I'm Smart! I Taught Myself My Times Tables.* She has given her permission to share this example of her method in this book.

Objective

In this program, numbers become characters, each with its own name, color, sound, and drawing. Each number/character has its own visual space on a tic-tac-toe grid. This gives the child a unique, visual picture of each fact.

Instructions

Each multiplication fact is taught through a short story about the two characters representing the numbers being multiplied together. The story is presented in both oral and visual form. The story always ends with a "punch line" that rhymes with the answer.

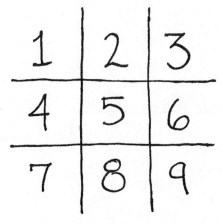

For example, if you want the child to learn 4 x 6 = 24, have them draw a large tic-tac-toe grid on the playground with the numbers 1, 2, 3 across the top; 4, 5, 6 across the middle; and 7, 8, 9 across the bottom. Let the children play on the grid for a couple of days. This gives them a kinesthetic and visual knowledge of the placement of the numbers on the grid.

Back in your classroom, have the students listen to the following story, either read by the teacher or played on the audiotape. Here is the story for 4 x 6 = 24. "4 Roar and 6 Swan have entered the tug-o-war contest at their company picnic. Each is captain of one team. After much pulling and tugging, 6 Swan is getting tired; her muscles are starting to hurt. She complains to 4 Roar, 'This tug-o'-war makes me 'plenty sore'; 'plenty sore' sounds like 'twenty-four' so 4 x 6 is 24."

Have your students chant the rhyme and clap in rhythm.

Give your students half of a standard sheet of colored paper, cut horizontally. Now, ask your students to draw their interpretation of a lion whose roar comes out in the shape of an orange 4 (4 Roar) and of a purple swan shaped like a 6 (6 Swan). Have them draw a rope between the mouths of the characters as in the drawing below.

"This tug-o'-war makes me

PLENTY SORE!"

Now complete the rest of the multiplication facts in the same fashion as this drawing. Have the students make books that you secure with brads or yarn, so they can add one or more facts per week depending on their age.

As students study the facts in their books, encourage them to hold each fact in their visual memory position and both trace and say the fact aloud, while relying on the mental snapshot of the fact for the test. Play Mozart or other music you have chosen as students draw their facts in their books.

MENTAL-IMAGERY EXERCISES

Objective

This exercise will help students create a more visual strategy for solving word problems.

Instructions

Write out a number sentence using numbers such as 7 x 8, or 4(7 x 8), if the students are older. Have them create and illustrate a story problem that reflects the number sequences. Have them create a picture map of their story. Tell them to hold the picture map up in their visual-memory location, and write the fact or problem in their story from memory. Have them share their picture maps with the class.

Objective

This exercise will help students create a more visual strategy for solving word problems.

Instructions

Have students look up (in their visual memory location, of course) and visualize a problem such as, "If I put five polar bears in pink bathing suits on my airplane, but one leaves before we take off, how many are left?" Or, use a prediction problem like "Susie's dog just had eight puppies. Five are black, two are red, and one is white. They are all in the same box. If she lets me choose one of them (while I am wearing a blindfold), what color am I most likely to get?"

Objective

The objective of this exercise is to help children recognize and visualize the same figure, no matter how it is turned in space.

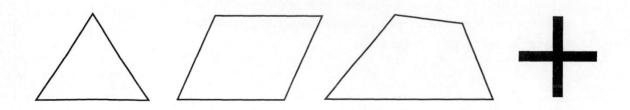

Instructions

Draw a triangle, parallelogram, trapezoid, and plus sign on a large sheet of white paper. On another sheet of paper the same size, draw the same figures, but rotate or turn them in other directions. On this second drawing, add a capital T and capital K to these figures and turn them on their sides. Put all figures in a different order than they appeared on the first paper. Hold the first sheet up in front of the class. Let the students look at it for about one minute. Then take it away and hold up the second sheet of paper. Ask the children to select which shapes were among those found on the paper they first looked at.

Chapter 6

Math Facts Mastery

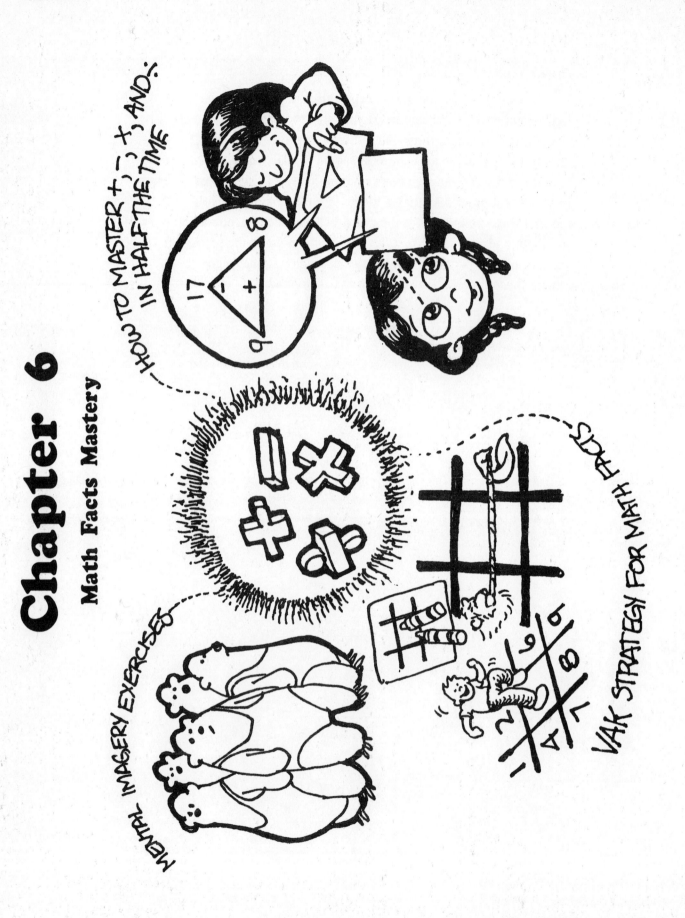

HOW TO MASTER +, −, ×, AND ÷ IN HALF THE TIME

MENTAL IMAGERY EXERCISES

VAK STRATEGY FOR MATH FACTS

Chapter 7
Mind Matters

In This Chapter

- **Picture Maps for Higher Grades**

- **How to Create a Picture Map**

- **Studying with Picture Maps**

- **Other Uses for Picture Maps**

Maps
for Higher Grades

*O**ne of the best ways I know of to
increase retention and boost grades
is to use picture maps. Picture maps make
it easy to learn and organize large amounts
of information and easily take the place of
traditional note-taking formats. You will
notice that picture maps are included at
the end of each chapter in this book as a
pictorial way of organizing and summarizing
the content.*

We have Tony Buzan, trainer and author, to thank for the invention of the Mind Map (picture map as we'll call them here) as a graphic way to organize and create visual images of new material to be learned. A picture map arranges material around a central idea (Buzan 1993). Buzan studied the three most common methods for note-taking during lectures and then tested each:

Associations play a dominant role in nearly every mental function, and every word and idea has numerous links attaching it to other ideas and concepts.

- Writing a complete transcript
- Writing a summary
- Writing key words only

The complete transcript method produced the worst results; the key-word method yielded the best results. Students using their own key words remembered information the best.

Picture maps make good use of the fact that the brain learns through associations and pictures. Associations play a dominant role in nearly every mental function, and every word and idea has numerous links attaching it to other ideas and concepts.

Picture Map Advantages

- allows you to learn more in less time
- improves memory and concentration
- fosters better organizational skills
- jump-starts creativity— encourages divergent thinking
- is aligned with brain-based learning
- fosters more efficient, whole-brain learning
- creates links between subjects
- makes learning more fun

Picture maps take on basically the same structure as memory itself, as shown by brain researchers (Ornstein 1991).

As I wrote this book, I used picture maps extensively to organize my thoughts and outline each chapter. I found that they inspired me and helped generate new ideas as I looked at them. Instead of using traditional, uninviting, and, frankly, boring outline forms, your students will be fired up about their note-taking and studying when you share picture maps with them. Have your students read their texts and create picture maps as they read. Every time they read or hear something that seems interesting or important, have them add the idea to their picture map.

HOW TO CREATE A PICTURE MAP

Objective

This exercise will help students create a more visual strategy for solving word problems.

Materials

- ► large sheets of unlined paper or light-colored construction paper—use in a horizontal (landscape) direction for more space
- ► thin-tipped colored markers or pencils

Instructions

Picture maps can be as elaborate or as simple as you wish. For example, to write this chapter, I put the words "picture maps" in a circle in the center of the page. I added lines around the main focus for new ideas as I thought of them. Then I made shapes such as hearts, squares, rectangles, stars, and so on for each category, attached to those lines drawn. In each shape, I put an image of what the information reminded me of (making associations, see page 57) and a few words connected to the image.

Picture-Mapping Chapters in a Text

Objective

To create a picture map to better understand a chapter

Instructions

Have your students look over the chapter to create an image in their minds of what the chapter is about. Then have them draw this central focus image in the center of the page. This can be in the form of an illustration, or a drawing placed inside a circle or other figure. Use lots of color and humor whenever possible, as this strengthens the memory process.

Have the class then look at each subsection of the chapter and draw lines from the central idea of the chapter around the page in clockwise direction. Keep equal spacing between the lines. Have them place a few words on the lines as they discuss and/or read more about the topic. The words can be placed directly on the line or diagonally.

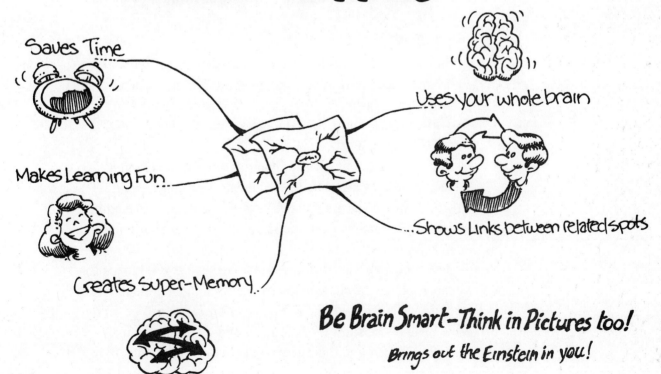

Picture Mapping

Saves Time

Uses your whole brain

Makes Learning Fun

Shows Links between related spots

Creates Super-Memory

Be Brain Smart—Think in Pictures too!
Brings out the Einstein in you!

Instruct the students to ask questions about each section in the chapter to determine what is most important to remember. Who, what, where, when, why, and how questions will promote new ideas for them to place on their picture map. Now, the students will create images of the ideas they determine to be most important. Have them connect each image with a couple of words that are related, by asking, "What does this remind me of?"

> *Brief is best. A picture map should include only a few well-chosen words with connected images.*

Brief is best. A picture map should include only a few well-chosen words with connected images. The images will trigger the words. The images should be colorful and meaningful to the individual student.

Studying with Picture Maps

Objective

Picture maps can strengthen the memory pathways in the brain.

Instructions

Adding as many senses to a picture map as possible will help strengthen memory pathways in the brain. When you add color, humor, sound, music, imagery, and associations to the map, students will accelerate their understanding and memory of what is on the map.

Students can create picture maps as you lecture about a subject, or as the class discusses elements of a chapter or lesson. Picture maps are a way to encourage the understanding of the relationship between the sections in a chapter and the main concept.

Once the maps are finished (you may have several maps for a chapter), have the students place the maps in their visual memory location (up to the left or up to the right) and begin to make mental snapshots of the images and words on the map. Have them go around their map clockwise and read what they have written aloud or silently, while still holding the map above eye level.

I have found that playing music while the class draws their picture maps can make this process even more powerful and enhance the effectiveness. Students learn to link a certain type of music with their creative and memory abilities, so I play the same music each time they study their picture maps before a test. See Resources listing (page 135) for music recommendations.

> *Picture maps are a way to encourage the understanding of the relationships between the sections in a chapter and the main concept.*

OTHER USES FOR PICTURE MAPS

As you become more experienced at creating and using picture maps you will discover that there are unlimited applications for the process. Here are just a few:

Organizing a Project

1. Many projects (such as writing a book report, studying for finals, or creating a plan) can overwhelm students in the beginning. Picture-mapping may eliminate this feeling, because it "chunks" the project into smaller pieces that are more manageable. It takes only a few minutes to organize an entire project using a picture map.

Brainstorming

2. Brainstorming is the kind of free-flowing activity that breeds high levels of creativity. Brainstorming was initially developed by Alex Osborn (1948), co-founder of an advertising firm. Osborn used brainstorming to develop creativity as early as 1939, and believed that a

critical aspect of business success was the ability to think "outside the box." When students brainstorm in the classroom, all judgment is suspended as ideas are written down. They will be producing quantity, seeking improvement, and achieving quality at the end of the process. Brainstorming can be used as a tool, with one classmate writing everything down on a large piece of butcher paper or the chalkboard as the other students call out unedited ideas.

Cooperative Projects

3. When a whole class or a small group creates a project, a picture map can be developed out of several pieces of paper. Several people can write one idea on a smaller sheet, and then put them all in the middle of a table. Other students can come up, take one sheet at a time, and write one or two more ideas related to the one chosen. At the end, a couple of students can create a picture map of the whole group's ideas. What a great way to encourage cooperative learning!

Writing

4. Using picture maps can quickly eliminate writer's block. Mapping encourages organization of the paper, article, or book, as ideas more easily flow from one another. Have students place the main idea in the middle—choose a noun or concept. Simply attach words around the idea as they come. Each word will trigger more. Pictures can be added later. Eventually, your students will settle on one or more of the words; soon they will have a topic to develop.

Journaling

5. Picture maps can also be used for journaling and developing students' ability to write down their thoughts in a unique format. Here are a few topics to get your students started:

> ▶ values
>
> ▶ success
>
> ▶ heart
>
> ▶ flower
>
> ▶ learning
>
> ▶ inspiration
>
> ▶ time
>
> ▶ pet
>
> ▶ kindness
>
> ▶ friendship
>
> ▶ helping
>
> ▶ overcoming obstacle

Chapter 7
Mind Matters

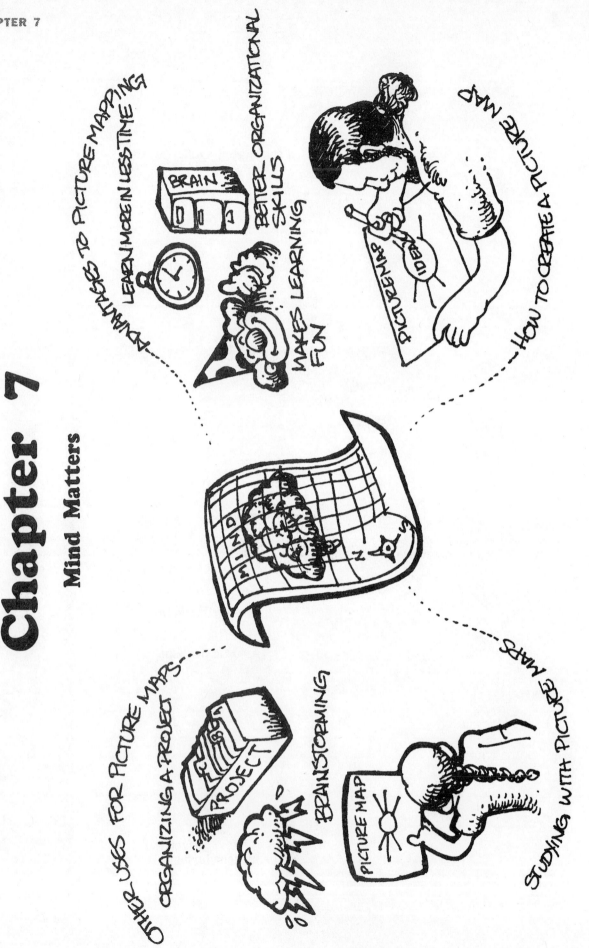

Chapter 8
Magnificent Memory Strategies

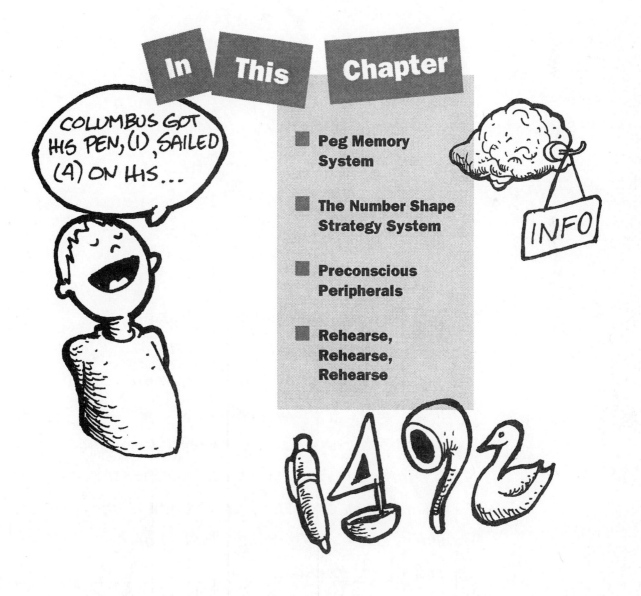

In This Chapter

- **Peg Memory System**

- **The Number Shape Strategy System**

- **Preconscious Peripherals**

- **Rehearse, Rehearse, Rehearse**

COLUMBUS GOT HIS PEN, (1), SAILED (4) ON HIS...

INFO

Peg
Memory System

When we understand how learning occurs through pictures and associations, we know that information we "input" into our brains, using pictures and associations, can be easily retrieved using the same formula. We then have access, better known as memory. Once information is input, memory is simply knowing where to look to recall the information.

We learned in chapter 1 that our brain works best using pictures with association. As an experiment, try to recall what you were wearing two days ago. Your brain does one or two things to help you remember. First, you may access a picture of yourself immediately and easily remember what you were wearing. Or, if you need to think for a moment, several things may pop into your mind that you associated with what you were wearing. These would help you recall the exact kind of clothing you had on.

Once information is input, memory is simply knowing where to look to recall the information.

You might remember where you were, and that triggers your memory. Perhaps you think of what you were doing to remember whether you had any special reason to wear a certain kind of clothing. Both of these things are known as associations—one thing reminded you of another.

The ancient Greeks and Romans often had elaborate memory contests to impress their fellow men with their "feats." Over 2,000 years ago they used several systems, all based on associations and pictures, which are now validated by brain research on how memory works.

Since our teaching and testing system relies so heavily on what students can recall, teaching your students memory techniques will reward them with better memories and higher self-esteem.

Since our teaching and testing system relies so heavily on what students can recall, teaching your students memory techniques will reward them with better memories and higher self-esteem. You can boost both your students' and your own success by giving them reliable, long-term strategies.

Let your students know that there is no such thing as a poor memory, only an "untrained" one. You and your students' memories will work like magic when you use a few, proven memory systems.

Memory Pegs

Objective

When you want your students to remember things in order—for example, the planets, days of the week, parts in an essay, a speech, steps to solve a math problem, and so on—you can use this ancient, proven peg-memory system.

1. .... Bun .... Mercury

2. .... Shoe............. Venus

3. .... Tree .... Earth

4. .... Door .... Mars

5. .... Hive .... Jupiter

6. .... Sticks .... Saturn

7. .... Heaven .... Uranus

8. .... Gate............. Neptune

9. .... Sign .... Pluto

Instructions

Look around the room you are in and see if there is a picture hanging on the wall. Think of a memory peg like the hook in your brain where you will hang what you want to remember. This system is reported on and adapted from Colin Rose's book, *Accelerated Learning* (1997) and Tony Buzan's *Use Both Sides of Your Brain* (1991).

Reinforce that they place this image on their visual memory screen.

To recall the planets in order, have your students "memorize" the pegs. Make an overhead of page 104, with the pegs and planets. Place it on your overhead and cover the planets.

Ask your students what they notice about the pegs and the numbers across from them. They will say the pegs rhyme with the numbers they are next to.

Then, have your students sit in their success position and begin to say the numbers and pegs aloud: "1 Bun, 2 Shoe, 3 Tree, 4 Door, 5 Hive, 6 Sticks, 7 Heaven, 8 Gate, 9 Sign." Have them repeat the process much louder and, again, in a whisper. Then have them close their eyes as you say the numbers aloud. Ask them to raise their hands high in the air if they know the rhyming peg. This way you can check for knowledge without students knowing if their friends know the answer or not. This may give them a sense of security.

Next, your students will need to make associations for the planets. Have them ask: "What does this remind me of?" In this case, ask them what the word, "mercury," reminds them of, other than the planet. They may say a car, the mythical winged god, or a thermometer.

Then ask them what "bun" reminds them of. Be sure they look up into their visual memory position and get a clear image of "bun." To verify they are doing this, ask things like, "does it have sesame seeds on it?" Or, ask if they thought of another kind of bun, such as a hot dog bun, a cinnamon sticky bun, or a hair bun. Whatever they thought of, have them create colorful images of it and look upward into their visual-memory position with it.

Finally, either on paper or in their visual memory "screen" position, have them connect both the mercury and the bun together in a single, humorous, colorful image.

Next, have them close their eyes, and ask "What is planet 1?" They will think of 1, the peg bun, and see *mercury* connected to the *bun*. They will quickly know that planet 1 is Mercury.

Then repeat the process with the other numbers, pegs, and associated images.

As they draw or place their images in their visual-memory location, play some of the music recommended in the Resources listing (see page 135) to anchor the learning with another modality.

> *Many of your students who are not visual learners do not naturally make pictures, and this is a wonderful way to show them how.*

After reviewing to see that your students know the planets in order, let them know you are giving them a written test. Have fun with this and remind them that they now have a strategy to rely on—their magic memory screen.

I often use this strategy in my teacher-education courses and teachers get first-hand experience of its power. Before we begin the exercise, I run around the room asking teachers to tell me, "What is planet 6, what is planet 2, what is planet 8?" I give them very little time to answer and when they don't know, I assure them that the peg memory strategy above will allow them to know the answers very rapidly for the "test."

The teachers are amazed at their success. Your students will experience the same thing.

A note to teachers who are highly visual learners: Are you wondering why you would go through this kind of exercise with your students? Are you thinking it might take too much time? Remember that you naturally make associations and pictures in your mind so quickly that you are hardly even aware of it. Many of your students who are not visual learners do not naturally make pictures, and this is a wonderful way to show them how.

Have your students try this strategy when you will be testing them on something that they have to remember in order—they'll shine!

> *Using imagination can make learning numbers easy and fun.*

THE NUMBER-SHAPE SYSTEM

Objective

When you want your students to remember numbers, dates, addresses, and so on, you can use what is called a number-shape system. This will speed up their learning and give them more free time for inquiry-based learning. Using imagination can make learning numbers easy and fun. Your students will be imagining each number in a special shape. Then when they want to remember dates, they will make up a story that goes with the shape of the number.

Instructions

Imagine each number to be in the following shapes:

Have the students draw pictures of the shapes each number represents—or you can make a poster of these pictures for them. Now they can make connections with pictures of the numbers and the shapes. They will do this by making up a story. This is a very efficient memory strategy for parents and teachers as well.

> *Link that association with big and bright pictures and memory will be truly enhanced.*

Repeat the numbers and their shapes out loud a couple of times before the students make up the story. Make sure that students are looking up at the numbers and shapes and not down toward the desk. Now have them make up a story.

For example, perhaps you want the students to remember a date in history. Take 1492 for example, when Columbus sailed to America.

They might create a story like this: Columbus got his pen, (1) sailed (4) on his ship, while smoking a (9) pipe; then he saw a swan (2) who led him to America. The story will easily translate back to the actual date and event you want to remember. Pen is the 1, sail is the 4, 9 is the pipe, and 2 is the swan. 1492 can be easily retrieved and recalled. The more humorous and unique you make your story, the easier it is to remember. Your story does not need to make sense.

Remembering telephone numbers and addresses works the same way. Simply recall the shapes of the numbers, which remind you of the actual numbers.

It is helpful to know that all memory strategies make use of the same things, pictures with connections or associations. Whenever you ask your students to remember anything such as dates or things in order, be sure to ask them what each thing reminds them of in order to get a strong association. Link that association with big and bright pictures and memory truly will be enhanced.

Preconscious Peripherals

Objective

When you want students to be reminded of their learning both as they enter the classroom and during the class session, place objects and images around the room related to what is being taught. You need not even make reference to these items for students to relate them to their learning.

Instructions

These materials are placed around the room and connected to the lesson plan. They can be anything that will affect the five senses. The objects encourage assimilation, connecting new information to previously known information. If your students should mentally "wander" during a lesson, what they will see as they look around your room will continue to reinforce what you are teaching.

Before students enter your classroom, put out welcome mats and welcome signs that include positive "I-can" statements. These help set the success tone for the class.

Rehearse, Rehearse, Rehearse

Objective

If your students do not review as they learn, they will only put the new information into short-term memory, quickly to be lost. Rehearsing newly learned material actually strengthens and

Rehearsing newly learned material actually strengthens and physically changes pathways in the brain and will make retrieval easier later on.

> *Good breaks are to stretch, exercise to cross the mid-line of the body to activate both brain hemispheres, and even dance to upbeat music.*

physically changes pathways in the brain and will make retrieval easier later on.

In his book, *Master It Faster*, author Colin Rose shows that the way in which students review their studies can at least double recall (Rose 1999). The cycle is to learn, review, sleep, review. Since many studies reinforce the fact that students remember most at the beginning and the end of a session, plan your lessons so that students take frequent breaks. Have several beginnings and endings in your lessons. Good breaks are to stretch, exercise to cross the mid-line of the body to activate both brain hemispheres, and even dance to upbeat music.

Instructions

Have students review material after one hour, one day, one week, and one month. Using music during learning and rehearsal will also help your students, their physiology, and their memories. The use of music reinforces learning by providing anchors to another sense and fostering an optimum learning state. When there is no music during high mental activity there will higher (beta) wave frequency, increased blood pressure, increased heart rate and muscle tension, as compared to these measures during less-demanding activities. When you add classical music (with no words) during high mental activity, the brain wave frequency decreases, thus lowering blood pressure,

> *The use of music reinforces learning by providing anchors to other sense and creating optimum learning states.*

slowing the heart rate, relaxing the muscles, and putting the learner in a better state for learning (Miles 1997).

The secret to an excellent lifelong memory, thus, is to expose yourself and your students to new ideas and associations—create alternative ways of doing everyday tasks, take new courses, and become involved with your new learning. Make it meaningful and relate it to something you already know.

Chapter 8

Magnificent Memory Strategies

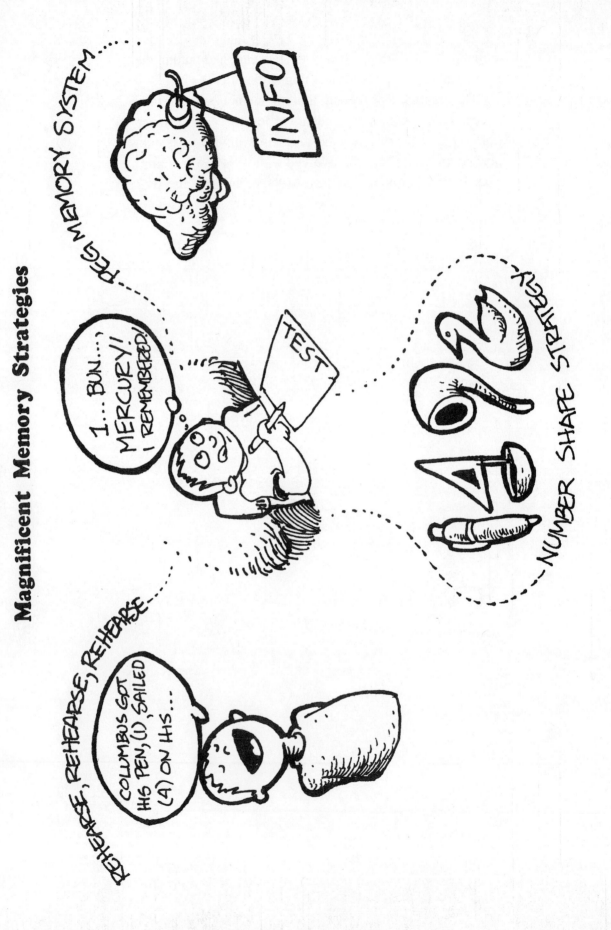

Chapter 9
Brain Smart~Body Smart

In This Chapter

- **Tips for Every Student's Success**

- **Belief, Body, Association, and Pictures**

- **How Nutrition Affects Learning**

- **The Learning Environment**

- **Dissolving Learning Blocks**

Tips
for Every
Student's Success

*H*elping students succeed means looking
at the needs of the whole child. Several
factors need to be considered including
health, safety, environment, and beliefs. The
following are some helpful tips you can use
right away to assist your students on their
road to learning success.

BELIEF, BODY, ASSOCIATION, AND PICTURES

As you design your lesson plans, always keep in mind the foundations of learning. *Belief, body, association,* and *pictures* (BBAP) are the four foundations on which I believe successful learning is built. When you include each of these in your lessons, your students will accelerate their learning abilities.

▶ *Belief*—In order for a student to develop a belief that he or she is successful and can learn, he or she must first experience success. As you plan your lessons and introduce new concepts, build in a match between learning styles and testing styles. The success your students experience leads to a belief

> *When you try out the new ideas in this book (or others), chunk down the learning task so that students start with smaller portions, to assure success.*

that they can be successful. When you try out the new ideas in this book (or others), chunk down the learning task so that students start with smaller portions, to assure success. In spelling, for example, give shorter lists of words in the beginning and build up to the usual number on your list. When first learning the new math facts strategy, suspend timed tests. Give your students a chance to get used to success before measuring the speed with which they can write their facts. This way, the students build a foundation of success and will be excited to try new things, knowing there is a strategy for learning each of them.

▶ *Body*—When your students are slumped over, they do not radiate success, internally or externally. Use the success position, described in chapter 4, to help your students get their bodies ready for success.

▶ *Association*—The brain creates associations naturally, and you will want to make association a conscious process for your students. Whenever you create a lesson, use what brain research says about learning and memory

to make it more powerful. In every subject area, have students ask themselves, "What does this remind me of?" to create an association in their brains. They can make associations based on sounds of the new word to be learned in vocabulary, or link new learning with past successes, events, and pictures in their lives. They can also learn to create new associations for the future. Teach them new phrases, such as "testing is fun when I know I have the strategies to do well." If the students are younger, they may like to use phrases like "I love testing, because I know how!"

▶ *Pictures*—When you want to guarantee learning success, have your students look up into their visual memory screen and recall pictures of what they learned with the associations they created. The brain learns best with pictures and associations. Classic brain/memory experiments, done by A. Pavio between 1969 and 1986, reveal that we recall best in images. Just for a moment, think of your oven at home. Did you recall the letters *o,v,e,n*, or did you see an image in your mind? During recall, use images frequently.

HOW NUTRITION AFFECTS LEARNING

Have you ever noticed a difference in your students' behavior right after Halloween because they have had too much refined sugar? How about Valentine's Day or just before the holidays? Do your students seem more active or even "hyperactive?"

The link between what children eat, how they behave, and their learning abilities deserves our attention as we search for new ways to help them achieve. This is something that both schools and teachers are in a position to address directly. Even though we may not think of food and learning as linked, there is a large body of scientific research to substantiate the connection.

When children come to school without food or with only sugary snacks in their stomachs, their systems cannot possibly function at optimum levels for their best performance in the classroom. Their brain is being robbed of the nutrients it needs when they are hungry or "running on sugary snacks" (Crook 1991; Carper 2000).

I recommend to teachers that they ask their students to keep a diary of what they eat during the week along with notes about how they feel and how they perform in the classroom. Ask them to notice whether they are tired, get head-aches, stomachaches, or runny noses. Each of these symptoms can be related to what they have eaten, and might impair learning and the skills needed during test taking.

> *The link between what children eat, how they behave, and their learning abilities deserves our attention as we search for new ways to help them achieve.*

In my book, *What's Food Got To Do With It? 101 Natural Remedies for Learning Disabilities,* I reported on the largest study ever done on the relationship between food and learning. It took place in the New York City public schools over a four-year period. Over one million students raised their national test scores 41 percent when the school cafeterias made changes in the kind of food they served. The cafeterias eliminated artificial colors, flavors, preservatives, like BHA and BHT, and reduced the amount of sugar.

Before and after the study, students took a national test to assess their progress. The study results were reported in the *International Journal of Biosocial Research* (1991). The New York City public schools raised their mean national academic performance percentile ranking from 39.2 percent to 54.9 percent in four years. Many more recent studies have appeared in various medical journals to validate the link between nutrition and learning.

Another study, done in 1986, suggests a connection between diet and delinquent behavior. Steven J. Schoenthaler, a

Choose rewards other than sugar. This will help eliminate the connection between comfort and food, and may save some children from a lifetime battle with obesity.

California State University criminologist, gave 26 institutionalized juvenile delinquents either a multivitamin-mineral supplement or a placebo for 13 weeks (Schoenthaler 1986). These children took the Wechsler Intelligence Scale for Children. Their blood was also measured for concentration of the supplements. The nonverbal scores on the IQ test went up an average of six points. One child's IQ score went up an astonishing 25 points, from 117 to 142. Further, the blood levels of the nutrients increased just as the IQ levels did, indicating that their bodies needed the vitamins and minerals.

More research is needed, but these studies and many more represent a developing field that can be of value to educators in helping students achieve.

In his book, *Healing through Nutrition,* Melvyn Werbach, M.D., claims that sugar can interfere with learning by increasing adrenaline levels. He notes a Yale study in which children had a dramatic rise in blood adrenaline after eating the equivalent of two frosted cupcakes for breakfast. The increase of adrenaline may cause anxiety, irritability, reduce concentration, and interfere with learning (Werbach 1993).

Some educators claim to have noticed a connection between students who take Ritalin or Dexedrine and also eat large quantities of sugar, high-fat foods, and other items that may be deemed unhealthy. Many school nurses I have spoken with have indicated they see a trend developing in this area.

During my years in the classroom, I noticed that many educators are increasingly asking parents to have their children medically evaluated, in order to consider drug therapy to control the students' classroom behavior problems. As new medical research identifies dangers and possible side effects of such drugs, I believe teachers and parents should explore other alternatives before turning to medicating their children to control behavior and enhance their academic performance.

THE LEARNING ENVIRONMENT

As school districts across the nation scramble to improve student-performance levels, they are trying alternative teaching methods, new materials, improved teacher training, mentor teacher programs, smaller classes, longer school years, Saturday sessions, and much more. However, in this search, many districts have not yet taken a close look at the physical classroom environment where their students spend so much time. Both student achievement and student behavior can be improved with some careful attention to the student learning space.

I believe teachers and parents should explore other alternatives before turning to medicating their children to control behavior and enhance their academic performance.

*H*ere are some recommendations regarding food and improving learning performance:

■ I have discovered that students who eat protein before exams have a higher energy level and are more alert. When they eat carbohydrates such as breads, pastas, and sugary cereals, they tend to become tired and sluggish. *Hint:* Eating peanuts or raw almonds (have parents send them in with their children, or bring them yourself) about 20 minutes before exams may help students think better and faster. Soaking the almonds all night in spring water will make them taste even better, as they lose their bitterness. Nuts supply choline and lecithin, building blocks of neurotransmitters in the brain that are needed for memory. *Check to make certain that students have no allergies to these before serving.*

■ Choose rewards other than sugar. This will help eliminate the connection between comfort and food, and may save some children from a lifetime battle with obesity.

■ Ask school personnel to reevaluate whether the money raised through the sale of colas and candy at school is worth the price the children may pay in terms of poor health and decreased learning abilities. While these machines may produce much-needed revenue, they teach students poor nutritional habits and encourage high levels of sugar consumption. High consumption of refined sugar, which may result in obesity, can contribute to type II diabetes. According to the American Diabetes Association, the incidence of type II diabetes, which historically had rarely been diagnosed in children, is now rapidly increasing in young children. In addition, eating too much sugar limits opportunities to obtain higher-quality nutrients. Some children may be more active after consuming sugar and may not be able to concentrate as well during class or during testing.

*A*s media reports of unhealthy, overweight children increase, take a look at what your school serves for breakfast and lunch. Are these meals healthy, or high in fat and refined sugar? Consider these points:

- Fast foods, such as French fries, are coated with sugar to make them brown better.

- Many fast foods and packaged foods have high levels of an unnatural substance, known as *hydrogenated oil,* which is linked with a large variety of health problems.

- Hydrogenated or trans fats can cause cell malfunctions that are bad for the body and brain. These fats are missing an electron and allow free radicals (which can cause diseases of all kinds) to roam throughout the body. While food manufacturers may increase their profits by increasing shelf life with hydrogenated fats, consumers' health may suffer.

- As children consume higher quantities of hydrogenated oils and fat, which are found in most packaged products on the market, their diets become dangerously deficient in the good fats known as *omega-3 fatty acids.* A Purdue University study (Stevens and Burgess 1996) concluded that many more behavior problems were reported in subjects with lower total omega-3 fatty acid concentrations. Also, more learning and health problems were found in boys, ages 6–12, with lower total omega-3 fatty acid concentrations. Eating salmon, canned albacore white tuna, sardines, herring, flax seeds, or flax oil will all help increase the levels of helpful omega-3 essential fatty acids in the system.

Daylight Improves Grades

Several recent studies have indicated that using natural lighting in the classroom can raise grades. For instance, a 1999 study done by the architectural consulting firm, Heschong Mahone Group, found that students who were taught in classrooms with more natural light scored as much as 25 percent higher on standardized tests than other students in the same school district (Cooper 1999).

This confirms the lifetime work of Dr. John Ott, a researcher who showed how fluorescent lighting (the kind found in nearly every classroom) distorts brain and nervous system functioning. The students in his studies who worked under fluorescent lights in the classroom were found to be tired, irritable, inattentive, and unruly. When full-spectrum lights were substituted, there was a significant reduction in behavioral problems, fewer learning disabilities, and improved academic performance. The students paid more attention to their teacher, showed more interest in their studies, and rarely needed discipline (Ott 1988).

When full-spectrum lights were substituted, there was a significant reduction in behavioral problems, fewer learning disabilities, and improved academic performance.

When I changed the lighting in both my classroom and my home to full spectrum (which more closely resembles natural light), I felt more clearheaded. I recommend that your school conduct some studies of their own by increasing full-spectrum, natural lighting in the classrooms. Observe whether there is a change in how both students and teachers feel and perform.

Can Electro-Pollution Affect Learning?

Another aspect in the physical learning environment to consider may be whether electromagnetic field (EMF) exposure impairs learning, health, or contributes to learning problems. Although studies are not conclusive and researchers often disagree, electromagnetic fields, produced from any electrical device, are increasing in number. Since many schools are built near high-power lines or transformers, EMF exposure is an issue that deserves more attention.

If you notice that you or your students are more fatigued than you would like, get headaches while using computers, are bothered by the fluorescent lights in the classroom, and so on, too much EMF exposure may be partially to blame. If you would like more information on this subject, refer to the Resources listing (see page 136) at the end of this book.

> *Using humor and exaggeration with your students helps keep them in a resourceful learning state.*

DISSOLVING LEARNING BLOCKS

When students struggle with learning and performing well on the tests, they may exhibit behaviors known as learning blocks. This means they may try to avoid learning, lose their ability to attend to a task for very long, slump over in their chair, say negative things to themselves, or stop trying at all, because they regard themselves as "dumb" or "stupid." They are basing their opinion of themselves on previous negative experiences in school. A learning block places a student in an un-resourceful state for learning.

Emotions are strongly related to long-term memory and learning. Using humor and exaggeration with your students helps keep them in a resourceful learning state. Use the humorous exercises below to help get students into a more empowered state for learning. (Note: have fun with this and both you and the students will enjoy the process.)

Tell students that you want to create the same result that they have on a test. Mention that you want precise directions for how to do this. If their grades were low, say that you would like to know how this was done so you can share it with other students in your class who may want to do the same thing. Ask students the following questions:

"*__How__ did you do that?*"

"Please tell me the first thing I need to do to feel badly about myself and get a poor grade. How do I have to stand, how do I sit, what kind of look needs to be on my face? What do I have to think about as I study and what do I have to think about when I take my tests?"

You will have the students laughing at this point, and you can begin to get them to associate more empowering things with learning and testing. Whenever you tell your students they are going to have a test, be sure and connect the word to something humorous at the same time.

Do the same exercise when a child excels or succeeds at something in your classroom. Ask the same questions as above and create a recipe for success. You might want to involve your whole class and have them draw pictures of success recipes to display around the room.

" *How* did you do that?"

Chapter 9
Brain Smart—Body Smart

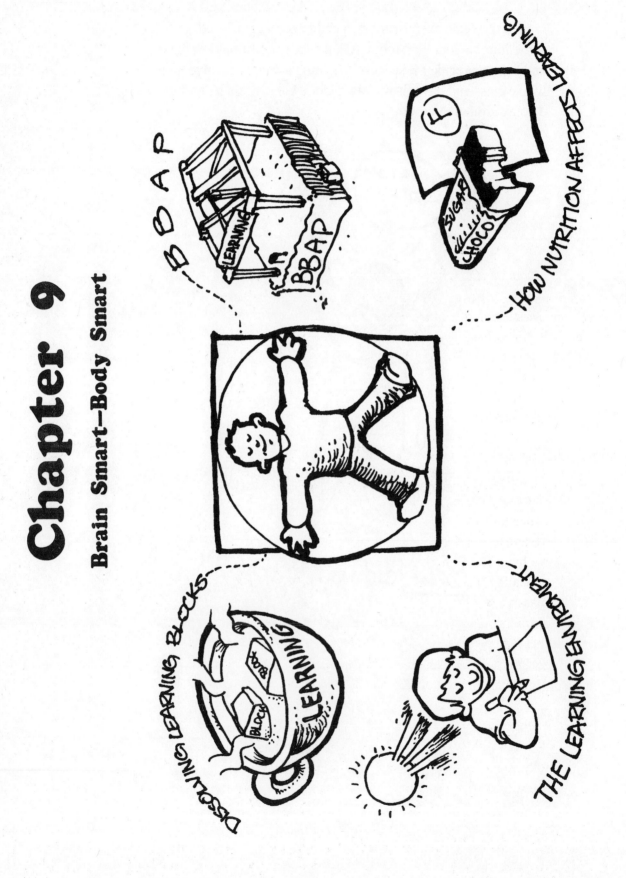

Epilogue
Some Thoughts
for the Thoughtful

In this increasingly complex and highly competitive world it is important to encourage and respect our children's unique gifts and special talents. We can begin to do this by building a solid, "whole-child" foundation for their learning and providing a safe and nurturing environment for them at home and at school.

The information and strategies in this book are a beginning toward a new paradigm in education—the ability to recognize what *is*, and offer our students success in the present, while we endeavor to try and revitalize the system as a whole. As a nation, we have set up parameters in the educational system that make massive change complex and extraordinarily slow. I believe that we have put the proverbial cart before the horse when we implement change at one end of the system, and continue to measure our students' progress with rulers that have not changed at the other end.

I believe that we have put the proverbial cart before the horse when we implement change at one end of the system, and continue to measure our students' progress with rulers that have not changed at the other end.

As a society, we are educating millions of students and understandably want to measure our results. Whether we take the shorter view of grades for that measurement, or the longer view of what our children and their grades contribute to our society, either one is myopic and shortchanges us all.

In every other aspect of society, success is measured by the ability to do the job. Sometimes that job is raising a child, sometimes it means the bottom-line profit in business, sometimes it's scoring the most points in a game, and sometimes it's winning an election. In all cases outside of school, we match the training to the expected outcome.

For now, it appears that we are confused about what outcomes we expect from our schools. If the outcome we want is to create a flexible, adaptable, creative workforce, we have a long way to go. If the outcome we want is to help our children keep abreast of society's technological advances, we know we have many changes to make when we are required to import labor personnel from other nations, just to stay competitive and fill the high-tech jobs. If the outcome is for happy, healthy individuals who love to learn and know how to learn for a lifetime, we're still a bit short of that as well.

As we think of how we want our educational system to look and what we want it to do, my hope is that the whole child will be our guiding light.

The meaning of education is emotionally laden and somewhat different for everyone. Yet, I believe that we all know we must change the system for the good of us all. As Leslie Hart said in *Human Brain and Human Learning*, "...we cannot expect to fit this new knowledge and its applications into the antique class and grade structure that Horace Mann brought back from Prussia almost 140 years ago."

As we think of how we want our educational system to look and what we want it to do, my hope is that the whole child will be our guiding light. Schools that have no relationship to where our children will go, who they will be, and what they are capable of will not help our children shine.

We have much new and significant understanding today about the brain, learning, health, safety, and even happiness. But our schools cannot do it all. We can begin, however, by using the knowledge we have. We can no longer turn out students without giving them the visual skills they need to be able to read. We can no longer conduct our lessons with total disregard for how children learn, giving our children pills to control their behavior, and feeding our students the foods we know are harmful, in the name of raising funds to keep our schools afloat.

The contradictions are many, but the possibilities are limitless. Teacher education sits on a volcano about to erupt with relevance for *how* children learn. Medical science is contributing extraordinary information to us about what keeps us well, how our brains function during learning and memory, and how our bodies respond to stress. Psychology tells us about learning states, the role of emotion in learning, and how people change. The fields of neurosciences, physics, and medicine tell us about environmental factors that can both hurt and heal us.

With all this available to us, I believe we have the capacity to listen. More importantly, we can use the information to design our schools, and bring our children soaring to extraordinary heights.

> *The contradictions are many, but the possibilities are limitless. Teacher education sits on a volcano about to erupt with relevance for* how *children learn.*

Bibliography

American Optometric Association News. May 1, 1989. "Special Report: Vision Problems and the Juvenile."

Bandler, R. and J. Grinder. 1975. *The Structure of Magic*. Palo Alto, Calif.: Science & Behavior.

Benton, David, et al. 1990. "Vitamin/Mineral Supplementation and Intelligence." *Lancet* 335 (8698): 1158–60.

Bradley, L. 1981. "The Organization of Motor Patterns for Spelling—An Effective Remedial Strategy for Backward Readers." *Developmental Medicine and Child Neurology* 23: 83–91.

Brewer, J. B., Z. Zhao, J. E. Desmond, G. H. Glover , and J. D. Gabrieli. 1998. "Making Memories: Brain Activity That Predicts How Well Visual Experience Will Be Remembered." *Science* 281(5380): 1185–87.

Buckner, R. L., M. E. Raichle, F. M. Miezin, and S. E. Petersen. 1996. "Functional Anatomic Studies of Memory Retrieval for Auditory Words and Visual Pictures." *Journal of Neuroscience* 16(19): 6219–35.

Buzan, T. 1991. *Use Both Sides of Your Brain*. New York: Penguin.

———. 1993. *The Mind Map Book*. New York: Dutton.

Carper, Jean. 2000. *Your Miracle Brain*. New York: HarperCollins.

Clark, J. M., and A. Pavio. 1991. "Dual Coding Theory and Education." *Educational Psychology Review* 3(3): 149–70.

Cooper, K. J. 1999. "Study Says Natural Classroom Lighting Can Aid Achievement." *Washington Post,* 26 Nov., p. A14.

Crook, William. 1991. *Help for the Hyperactive Child*. Jackson, Tenn.: Professional.

Diamond, M., and J. Hopson. 1998. *Magic Trees of the Mind: How to Nurture Your Child's Intelligence, Creativity, and Healthy Emotions from Birth through Adolescence*. East Rutherford, N. J.: Penguin.

DePorter, B. 1992. *Quantum Learning*. New York: Dell.

DePorter, B., M. Reardon, and S. Singer-Nourie. 1999. *Quantum Teaching*. Needham Heights, Mass.: Allyn & Bacon.

Druckman, D., and R. A. Bjork, eds. 1991. *In the Mind's Eye: Enhancing Human Performance*. Washington, D.C.: National Academy Press.

Earle, J. B. 1985. "The Effects of Arithmetic Task Difficulty and Performance Level on EEG Alpha Asymmetry." *Neuropsychologia* 23(2): 233–42.

Fisher, C. 1999. "Can You See the Board?" *Los Angeles Times*, March 26.

Frank, A. R., D. P. Wacker, T. Z. Keith, and T. K. Sagen. 1987. "Effectiveness of a Spelling Study Package for Learning-Disabled Students." *Learning Disabilities Research* 2: 110–18.

Garner, A. I., ed. 1999. "A Sports Vision Success Story. Greg Vaughn's Turnaround." *Sports Vision Journal*, Spring.

Grunau, R. V., and M. D. Low. 1987. "Cognitive and Task-Related EEG Correlates of Arithmetic Performance in Adolescents." *Journal of Clinical and Experimental Neuropsychology* (5): 563–74.

Guilford, J. P. 1950. "Creativity." *American Psychologist* 5: 444–54.

———. 1967. *The Nature of Human Intelligence*. New York: McGraw-Hill.

Gur, R. C., R. E. Gur, A. D. Rosen, S. Warach, A. Alavi, J. Greenberg, and M. Reivich. 1983. "A Cognitive-Motor Network Demonstrated by Positron Emission Tomography." *Neuropsychologia* 21(6): 601–6.

Haigler, K. O., C. Harlow, and A. Campbell. 1994. *Literacy behind Prison Walls*. Washington, D.C.: National Center for Educational Statistics, ED 377: 325.

Harris, K. R., S. Graham, and S. Freeman. 1988. "Effects of Strategy Training on Metamemory among Learning Disabled Students." *Exceptional Children* 54: 332–38.

Hart, L. A. 1991. *Human Brain and Human Learning*. Oak Creek, Ariz.: Books for Educators.

Heinke, M., and R. Greenburg. 1981. *Learning Related Visual Problems*. Reston, Va.: ERIC Clearinghouse on Handicapped and Gifted Children.

Iidaka T., N. Sadato, H. Yamada, and Y. Yonekura. 2000. "Functional Asymmetry of Human Prefrontal Cortex in Verbal and Non-Verbal Episodic Memory as Revealed by fMRI Brain Research." *Cognitive Brain Research* 9: 73–83.

Jensen, E. 1988. *Super Teaching*. Del Mar, Calif.: Turning Point.

Johnson, L. N. 1971. "I Was Nearly a Dropout." New York: *Family Circle Magazine*, March.

Johnson, R., D. N. Stratton, and J. Zaba. 1996. "The Vision Screening of Academically and Behaviorally At-Risk Pupils." *Journal of Behavioral Optometry* 7(2): 39.

Kimple, J. 1997. *Eye Q and the Efficient Learner.* Santa Ana, Calif.: OEP Foundation.

Markova, D. 1992. *How Your Child Is Smart: A Life-Challenging Approach to Learning.* Berkeley, Calif.: Conari Press.

McKim, R. 1997. *Thinking Visually?* White Plains, N.Y.: Dale Seymour.

Miles, E. 1997. *Tune Your Brain: Using Music to Manage Your Mind, Body and Mood.* New York: Berkeley.

National Assessment of Educational Progress. 1998. "The Nation's Report Card." Internet: http://nces.ed.gov/nationalsreportcard/reading/read_assess.achieve3.asp.

National PTA Conference. 1999. "Learning Related Vision Problems Education and Evaluation." Resolution adopted June 1999.

National Research Council. 1999. *How People Learn: Brain, Mind, Experience, and School.* Washington, D.C.: National Academy Press.

Optometric Extension Program Foundation, Inc. 1998. *Sports Vision: Giving Your Child the Visual Advantage.* Santa Ana, Calif.: Optometric Extension Program Foundation.

Ornstein, R. 1991. *The Evolution of Consciousness: The Origins of the Way We Think.* New York: Touchstone.

Osborn, A. 1948. *Your Creative Power: How to Use Imagination to Brighten Life and Get Ahead.* New York: Charles Scribner's Sons.

Ott, J. 1988. *Health and Light.* Greenwich, Conn.: Devin Adair Publishers.

Parker, S. 1989. *The Eye and Seeing,* rev. ed. New York: Franklin Watts.

Parnell, L. 1997. *Transforming Trauma: EMDR.* New York: Norton.

Pavio, A. 1969. "Mental Imagery in Associative Learning and Memory." *Psychological Review* 76: 241–63.

———. 1971. *Imagery and Verbal Processes.* New York: Holt Reinhart Winston.

———. 1986. *Mental Representations.* New York: Oxford.

Pavio, A., and I. Begg. 1981. *The Psychology of Language.* Englewood, N.J.: Prentice Hall.

Roediger, H. 1997. "Memory: Explicit and Implicit." Paper presented at the Symposium Recent Advances in Research on Human Memory. Washington, D.C.: National Academy of Sciences.

Rombouts, S. A., P. Scheltens, W. C. Machielson, F. Barkhof, F. G. Hoogenraad, D. J. Veltman, J. Valk, and M. P. Witter. 1999. "Parametric fMRI Analysis of Visual Encoding in the Human Medial Temporal Lobe." *Hippocampus* 9(6): 637–43.

Rose, C. 1999. *Master It Faster.* Las Vegas, Nev.: Accelerated Learning Institute.

Rose, C., and M. Nicholl. 1997. *Accelerated Learning for the Twenty-First Century.* New York: Dell.

Schoenthaler, S. J. 1986. "The Impact of a Low Food Additive and Sucrose Diet on Academic Performance in 803 New York City Public Schools." *International Journal of Biosocial and Medical Research*, 8(2): 185–95.

Shapiro, F. 1997. *EMDR: Eye Movement Desensitization and Reprocessing.* Harper-Collins. New York: Basic Books

Shapiro, S. 1992. "Vision and Juvenile Delinquency." *Eye Care Business* (March) 23-25. Norwalk, Conn.: Biscom.

Shelquist, J., and B. Breeze. 1971. *Resource Handbook for Development of Learning Skills.* Roseburg, Ore.: Educational Programmers.

Slingerland, B. H. 1996. *A Multi-Sensory Approach to Language Arts for Specific Language Disability Children.* Cambridge, Mass.: Educators Publishing Service.

Sousa, D. A. 1995. *How the Brain Learns.* Reston, Va.: National Association of Secondary School Principals.

Valett, R. 1974. *The Remediation of Learning Disabilities.* Belmont, Calif.: Fearon-Pitman Publishers.

Wagner, A. D., D. L. Schachter, M. Rotte, W. Koutstall, A. Maril, A. M. Dale, B. R. Rosen, and R. L. Buckner. 1998. "Building Memories: Remembering and Forgetting of Verbal Experiences as Predicted by Brain Activity." *Science* 281 (5380): 1188–91.

Walker, E., S. Wade, and I. Waldman. 1982. "The Effect of Lateral Visual Fixation on Response Latency to Verbal and Spatial Questions." *Brain and Cognition.* Oct 1(4): 399–404.

Waugh, N. C. 1963. "Immediate Memory as a Function of Repetition." *Journal of Verbal Learning and Verbal Behavior* 2: 107–112.

Werbach, M. 1993. *Healing through Nutrition.* New York: HarperCollins.

Zenhausern, R., and M. Kraemer. 1991. "The Dual Nature of Lateral Eye Movements." *International Journal of Neuroscience* Jan.–Feb. 56(1–4): 169–75.

Resources

For further information on reading improvement and visual training, reference the following resources.

TEACHING/LEARNING

The Center for New Discoveries in Learning, Inc.

▶ Teacher, Parent, and Corporate Workshops on Instant Learning® strategies to accelerate learning, raise grades, and improve standardized test scores

▶ Medical School Instant Learning® Seminars for Students and Faculty to raise medical board scores

▶ Individualized Activities Correction Kit (now known as I Read I Succeed Kit), covering a full range of visual-skills training exercises for students' reading success; can be used by teachers and parents

Pat Wyman, (800) 469-8653 or (707) 837-8180
E-mail: info@howtolearn.com
www.HowToLearn.com

Accelerated Learning Institute

▶ accelerated learning and accelerated language-learning courses, books, tapes

Peter Kenyon, (800) 874-7779
www.accelerated-learning.com and www.acceleratedlearning.com

Brain Gym

▶ instruction for improving teaching and learning through the science of movement

(800) 356-2109
www.braingym.org

Kaizen Training

▶ accelerated-learning training in England

Kim and Patrick Hare
www.kaizen-training.com

Homeschooling
- ▶ #1 homeschooling site on the Internet, providing support, advice, and curriculum products

  www.homeschool.com

S.O.I. Counseling and Testing Center and SOI Institute
- ▶ assistance with identifying learning abilities, remedial education, and career counseling

  www.soisystems.com

RESOURCES FOR READING AND VISION IMPROVEMENT
College of Optometrists in Vision Development (C.O.V.D.)
- ▶ nonprofit organization with free information on the critical link between vision and learning

- ▶ provides a complete resource directory of developmental optometrists who do vision therapy to help improve eyesight, reading, athletic abilities, and more

  www.covd.org

InfantSEE
- ▶ nonprofit organization for the prevention and early detection of vision problems

- ▶ resources for a lifetime of healthy vision for infants; the American Optometric Association (AOA) provides a Doctor Locator to find an InfantSEE doctor near you

- ▶ over 7,000 AOA-member optometrists have volunteered to serve as InfantSEE optometrists nationwide and provide free vision exams for infants

- ▶ former President Jimmy Carter is the honorary spokesperson for InfantSee

- ▶ please see the video on the InfantSEE Web site at www.infantsee.org

Parents Active for Vision Education (P.A.V.E.)
- ▶ nonprofit resource and support organization; free information on vision and learning

- ▶ *Vision in the Classroom* (35-minute video showing link between vision and classroom success)

- ▶ *Vision Alert: 20/20 Is Not Enough* (vision-training tool for parents and teachers)

  www.pavevision.org

Optometric Education Program Foundation (O.E.P.)
- ▶ nonprofit organization to help children and adults overcome vision problems

- ▶ lists of doctors who specialize in vision therapy

▸ *Classroom Visual Activities*, by Regina Richards (manual to enhance the development of visual skills)

▸ *Eyes on Track*, by Dr. Kristy Remick, Carol A. Stroud, and Vicki Bedes

(949) 250-8070
www.oep.org

VISION-SCREENING RESOURCES FOR SCHOOLS
New York State Optometric Association (NYSOA)
Vision-Screening Battery

▸ comprehensive vision-screening battery for school purchase; also offers the Keystone Telebinocular

Vision Training Products and others, (800) 348-2225
www.bernell.com

Titmus Vision Screener

▸ Vision-screening device for school purchase

Titmus Optical, Inc., (800) 446-1802
www.titmus.com

MUSIC RESOURCES
Tune Your Brain

▸ Mozart Effect CD series for learning; for classroom, work, or home use

www.HowToLearn.com/mozart.html

SUGGESTED WEBSITES
Electro-Pollution and Electro-Magnetic Fields

▸ resources to protect against and lessen effects of electro-magnetic fields

www.HowToLearn.com/qlink.html

Environmental/Physical Learning Space

▸ information and products on creating full-spectrum (natural) lighting sources

www.HowToLearn.com (free 52 Instant Learning® Tips)
www.HowToLearn.com/omega3.html

Society for Neuroscience

▸ http://www.sfn.org

RECOMMENDED READING

Should you have further interest in discovering more about the brain, learning, visual thinking, memory, and testing, here are some recommended readings.

Begley, S. 1997. "How to Build a Baby's Brain." *Newsweek* (Spring/Summer) 28–32.

Buzan, T. 1983. *Use Both Sides of Your Brain*. New York: E. B. Dutton.

Caine, G., R. Caine, and S. Crowell. 1999. *Mindshifts*. 2nd ed. Chicago: Zephyr Press.

Caine, R., and G. Caine. 1994. *Making Connections: Teaching and the Human Brain*. Menlo Park, Calif.: Addison-Wesley.

Cohen, D. 1996. *The Secret Language of the Mind*. San Francisco: Chronicle.

Dowling, J. E. 1998. *Creating Mind*. New York: W. W. Norton.

Dryden, G., and J. Vos. 1995. *The Learning Revolution*. Torrance: Calif.: Jalmar Press.

Goleman, D. 1995. *Emotional Intelligence*. New York: Bantam.

Hannaford, C. 1995. *Smart Moves*. Arlington, Va.: Great Oceans.

Howard, P. 2000. *The Owner's Manual for the Brain*. Austin, Tex.: Bard Press.

Jensen, E. 1998. *Teaching with the Brain in Mind*. Alexandria, Va.: ASCD.

Khalsa, D. S. 1997. *Brain Longevity*. New York: Warner.

Kimple, J. 1997. *Eye Q and the Efficient Learner*. Santa Ana, Calif.: Optometric Extension Program.

Kohn, A. 1993. *Punished by Rewards*. Boston: Houghton Mifflin.

Pert, C. B. 1997. *Molecules of Emotion*. New York: Scribner's.

Pinker, S. 1997. *How the Mind Works*. New York: W.W. Norton.

Posner, M., and M. Raichle. 1997. *Images of Mind*. New York: Scientific American Library.

Restak, R. M. 1994. *Receptors*. New York: Bantam.

———.1995. *Brainscapes*. New York: Hyperion.

Sylwester, R. 1995. *A Celebration of Neurons*. Alexandria, Va.: ASCD.

Index

A

Accelerating Children's Excellence in School, xiii
addition and subtraction 81-84
ADHD (Attention Deficit Hyperactive Disorder)
    and diet, 116
    and reading problems, 28-29, 30-31
    Ritalin use and, 118-119
associations, making
    brain learns by, 116
    teaching students process for, 115-116
auditory learners, x-xi, 4-5
    tell-tale traits, 5

B

body position, as relates to success, 115
brain research on learning, 12-13

C-D

classroom
    electromagnetic field (EMF), exposure to, 123
    importance of natural lighting in, 122
    typical (checklist), 38

E-F

education
    making positive changes in, 128-129
    moving to a new paradigm in, 127
    society's overview of, 127-128
electromagnetic field (EMF) exposure, 123
eye movements, looking up, 16-19
    research on, 17
eyesight
    20/20 vision is not good enough, 24-26

G-H

grades
    natural lighting may improve, 122
hyperactive students. *See* ADHD

J-K

juvenile delinquency
    link between poor diet and, 117-118
    link between vision problems and, 27
kinesthetic learners, x-xi, 4-5
    tell-tale traits, 5
    what works best for teaching, 6

L

LD/ADHD look-alikes, 23
learning
    and children, 2
    foundations of, 115-116
    how nutrition affects, 116-118
    using strategies to maximize, 13-16
learning blocks
    exercises to dissolve, 123-125
    to avoid learning, 123-125
learning disabilities
    and reading problems, 28-29, 30-31
learning environment, 119
    natural lighting in classroom, 122
learning styles, 3-6
    auditory learning, x, 4-6
    determining which style works, 7-9, 10
    kinesthetic, x-xi, 4-6
    visual learning, x, 4-6
    and written tests, 14-16

M

math
    addition and subtraction strategies, 81-84
    mental imagery exercises, 87-89
        word problems, 87-89
    multiplication and division strategies, 84-87
memory strategies, 101-112
    music as memory aid, 60, 110-111
    number-shape system, 107-108
    peg-memory system, 102-107
    preconscious peripherals, 109-111
    rehearsing newly learned material, 109-111

reviewing material, 109-111
mental imagery
    act of looking up, 16-17
    to help students with math, 87-89
    tips to help students recall, 18-19
    as tool to help students learn, 15-16
mnemonics, 64-65
modalities of learning, 3-5
multiple intelligences
    teaching vs. single-modality testing, xiii
    theory of, xii
multiplication and division strategies, 84-87
music
    classical music enhances learning, 110-111
    resources, 136
    using as memory aid, 60, 110-111

N

number-shape system, 107-108
nutrition
    fast foods and, 121
    how learning affected by, 116-118
    hydrogenated oils and trans fats, 121
    for improving learning, 120-121
    sugar's role in learning, 116-117, 120

P

peg memory system, 102-107
Personal Learning Styles Inventory, 7-9
phonics, and spelling, 70
picture (exercise), 23, 24-25
picture maps, 93-99
    advantages of, 93
    creating a, 94
    studying with, 96-97
    uses for, 95-99
        brainstorming, 97-98
        cooperative projects, 98
        journaling, 99
        organizing a project, 98
        writing, 98
problem students, xvi-xvii

R

reading
    inventory to assess visual skills, 39-44
    learning to read left to right, 36
    national reading proficiency levels, 29
    problems with, 28-29
    need more than good eyesight, 25-26
    visual skills and, 35
Ritalin use, 118-119

S

spelling
    expect success, 71, 72, 75, 76-77
    one student's story, 68-69
    phonics and, 70
    Super Speller strategy, 69-70, 71-75
    tied to self-esteem, 69
strategies
    to improve math skills, 81-87
    to improve spelling, 69-70, 71-75
    to improve vocabulary, 57-62
    to maximize learning, 13-16
success
    body position, 115
    when teaching spelling, 71, 72, 75,
      76-77
    letting students experience, 115
    taking tests, hints to help, 63

T

tests
    hints to help students be successful, 63
    visual strategies for written, 14-16

V-W

VAK (visual, auditory, and kinesthetic),
    85-87
vision
    school screening programs, 30-31,
      135-136
    links between school success and, 28
    problems, 26, 27
    training exercises, 45-47

    learned skill, 25-26
    20/20 isn't good enough, 24-26
visual learners, x, 4-5
    tell-tale traits, x, 5
    tips to help recall and learn, 18-19
    what works best for teaching, 6
visual memory
    act of looking up left or up right, 18-19
    strategies
        to improve spelling, 69-70, 71-75
        to improve vocabulary, 57-62
visual skills
    effects on reading, 35
    for academic success, 35, 37
    for typical classroom tasks, 38
    reading inventory to assess, 39-44
    screening equipment, 49-52, 135-136
    training to help students, 52-53
    picture associations, 115-116
visual stress
    reducing, 48-49, 53
vocabulary
    using mnemonics, 64-65
    picture association to improve, 57-62
Wyman Foundational Reading Skills
    Inventory, 40-44